Advance comments about *Losing Freedom*

My father was executed by firing squad in 1961 for his efforts to bring freedom back to Cuba, away from communist tyranny. Linden Blue was in prison with him and has never forgotten. He is telling part the experience he shared with my father and relating it to the present-day disaster of socialist authoritarian governments throughout history. Over half a Century has passed, my father did not die in vain believing that Freedom was worthy of the ultimate sacrifice.
Martica D. Trueba, daughter of Domingo Trueba

Losing Freedom nails one of the major problems this country faces. Linden Blue takes his personal experience and those of his co-prisoners just prior to the Bay of Pigs invasion and shows how policy failures and missed opportunities throughout history have stifled freedom. As a senior executive of a leading technology company he suggests how and why the future can be much better.
The Honorable Daniel S. Goldin, longest serving NASA Administrator under three US Presidents

No one has contributed more to the nation's security, with less desire for notoriety, than Linden Blue. Now he brings his technological sophistication to bear on America's current collectivist, statist temptations. This is a clarion call for fidelity to the rights-based individualism, and the spontaneous order of a market society, that have made America preeminent.
George F. Will, Author of "The Conservative Sensibility"

Linden Blue is one of America's most amazing and important entrepreneurs. In *Losing Freedom* he skillfully interweaves the riveting story of his capture and imprisonment in Castro's Cuba in 1961, with a discussion of the threats that human freedom faces today and in the future. The result is a powerful document that is well worth reading, especially by young people, and which will provoke debate for a long time to come.
Arthur Herman, Hudson Institute, author of "Freedom's Forge"

America's governmental system as framed by our founders drew on customs and practices from the classical world. The framers were inspired by perceived Greek and Roman political successes, along with Enlightenment ideas and English common law, and then they incorporated all of these beliefs into our Constitution and Bill of Rights. Their first principles continue to guide Americans in addressing the many problems of ensuring prosperity and peace in a rapidly changing world—even as classical freedom remains our most cherished and greatest asset. Linden Blue's engaging *Losing Freedom* will inspire young people both to understand and to cherish our most exceptional founding and its origins—a much needed reminder of what we must preserve in an age of increasing amnesia about who we were and must continue to be.

Victor Davis Hanson, Senior fellow, Hoover Institution and author "The Second World Wars"

Linden Blue is a highly regarded leader in aerospace technology and business development. As COO of Learjet he initiated development of the first commercial aircraft with winglets. More recently, as vice chairman of General Atomics, he was involved in development of the Predator drone which has revolutionized modern military combat. *Losing Freedom* is full of insights and is a cautionary tale about public policy that can spell the difference between peace and conflict, prosperity and privation.

Norman R. Augustine, Retired Chairman & CEO, Lockheed Martin Corp.

A deeply personal account, from a world-class entrepreneur, of the miracle that is modern prosperity and civil peace. As Linden Blue explains, that miracle rests on the foundations of the rule of law and commerce built by the west.

Heather Mac Donald, Manhattan Institute, author of "The War on Cops"

LOSING FREEDOM

Socialism and the Growing Threat to
American Life, Liberty and Free Enterprise

BY LINDEN BLUE
WITH LAURA DEE

Palmetto Publishing Group
Charleston, SC

Losing Freedom
Copyright © 2019 by Linden S. Blue

First Edition

Printed in the United States

Hardcover: 978-1-64111-631-2
Paperback: 978-1-64111-632-9
eBook: 978-1-64111-633-6

Dedication

To Domingo Trueba and Ñongo Puig, their families,
and all those in Cuba and elsewhere in the world
who are fighting against tyranny—in all its forms

"Let Freedom Ring"

(see my letter to Domingo Trueba's wife, October, 1961, page 168)

TABLE OF CONTENTS

DEDICATION $\cdots$ v

TABLE OF CONTENTS $\cdots$ vii

PREFACE and HISTORICAL CONTEXT $\cdots$ xi

INTRODUCTION $\cdots$ xvii

1. FREEDOM OR SOCIALISM? $\cdots$ 1

Why you can't have both, and what drives the uninformed attraction to socialism?

    A   Millennials and the "More Generous Safety Net" $\cdots$ 4

    B   The Rise of Democratic Socialism $\cdots$ 7

    C   The Hollywood Fantasy $\cdots$ 9

    D   How Socialism Leads to Loss of Freedom $\cdots$ 11

    E   The Slow Drift Away From Freedom $\cdots$ 14

    F   There is No "Both" $\cdots$ 17

    G   Socialism and the Assault on Free Speech $\cdots$ 25

    H   Lies and the Cycles of History $\cdots$ 28

2. WHAT CICERO KNEW $\cdots$ 30

Two thousand years of failed socialism

    A   Cicero was more prescient than he knew $\cdots$ 31

    B   Cry for Me, Argentina $\cdots$ 31

    C   Crisis in Venezuela $\cdots$ 35

    D   The Rise and Fall of the Berlin Wall $\cdots$ 39

    E   The Fall of Greece $\cdots$ 42

    F   In the Land of Mandela $\cdots$ 43

    G   Cicero and the Inevitable Socialist Destination $\cdots$ 44

3. HOW NOT TO HAVE A REVOLUTION · 46

The Failure of Cuban Communism

    A   Revolution and Repression · 48

    B   The Ex-Patriots Regroup: The Bay of Pigs · · · · · · · · · · · · · · · · 50

    C   The Cuban Missile Crisis ·52

    D   Khrushchev Blinks ·53

    E   A Cuban Connection to the JFK Assassination? · · · · · · · · · · · · ·53

    F   A World of Challenges · 54

    G   Cuba Today ·59

    H   Cuba—U.S. Relations ·65

    I   The Cuba—U.S. Risk ·67

    J   Cuba's Uncertain Future · 68

4. SWEDEN'S DECLINING FOUNDATION · · · · · · · · · · · · · · · · · · · 72

The Myth Of Swedish Socialism

    A   When Capitalism was King ·72

    B   The Capitalist Trust Fund ·73

    C   Does the "Nordic Model" Transfer? ·76

    D   Swedish Socialism in Decline · 77

    E   Failing to Compete ·81

    F   A Changing Sweden · 85

    G   The Impact of Immigration · 86

5. DID ATHENS GET IT RIGHT? · 89

Freedom, free enterprise, and the origins of democracy

    A   From Rome with Love: Individual Freedom Emerges · · · · · · · · · ·92

    B   The Debt We Owe The Brits: Magna Carta and Common Law · · · ·93

    C   A Country Founded on Ideals:

          The "Operating System" of the United States of America · · · · · · · · ·95

    D   A Constitutional Republic Is The Best System · · · · · · · · · · · · · ·101

    E   240 Years and Counting · 104

    F   Property Rights are a Hallmark of a Free Society. · · · · · · · · · · · · 107

    G   Americans experience the Soviet Union · · · · · · · · · · · · · · · · · ·114

    H   How Much Government is Enough? ·115

6. THERE IS NO THIRD WAY · 124

Why Free Enterprise Capitalism Works Better Than Any Other System

    A   What Drives Progress· 125

    B   A World Without Corporations· ·127

    C   Competition as the Great Stimulator of Progress · · · · · · · · · · · · · ·132

    D   "Creative Destruction· ·135

    E   Which Road: Serfdom or Prosperity? ·139

    F   Why Doesn't Free Enterprise Do Well in Popularity Polls? · · · · · · ·147

    G   The Challenge: understanding and preserving freedom · · · · · · · · · ·151

7. CHOOSING FREEDOM · 154

America at the Crossroads

    A   The Power of Choice ·155

    B   The Road of No Return ·156

    C   The Rising Tide of Freedom· ·157

APPENDIX · 162

GLOSSARY · 177

BIBLIOGRAPHY · 198

PREFACE
AND HISTORICAL CONTEXT

The seeds of civilization germinated some 5,500 years ago in Mesopotamia, where the first city-states arose in the Eastern Mediterranean—an area known as the fertile crescent, now made up of Iraq, Kuwait and parts of Turkey, Iran and Syria.

Five thousand-plus years may seem like a long time, but to put that in perspective, our earth was created roughly 4.5 billion years ago. Mankind itself has existed for more than 100,000 years. Civilization, as we think of it, is indeed a relatively recent development. Our 5,500 years of civilization, compared to the 4.5 billion years of the earth's life, is less than one hour out of an average person's 700,000 hours of expected life. So think of it this way, less than one hour out of your total life's 700,000 hour expectation (about 80 years), is the equivalent of the 5,500 years of civilization compared to the earth's life so far.

Perhaps the most striking aspect of those five or so civilized millennia, however, isn't their relative brevity; it's that for the vast majority of the time, nearly everyone was *poor*. Only tyrants living on the backs of others enjoyed good lives. There were exceptions, of course, but those exceptions tended to be short and relatively insignificant in the quest for a better life.

Even as recently as the 1600's, the famous British philosopher and historian Thomas Hobbes, described life as "solitary, poor, nasty, brutish and short." If anything, "short" was good news; life only lasted an average of 30-35 years, and for the vast majority of people those years were filled with suffering. Freedom was rare. Frustration with the inability to improve one's life overwhelmed the human spirit.

It was only during the last 200 years or so—a further, smaller fraction of mankind's existence—that most of human life consisted of more than a desperate effort to survive against the perversities of nature and the ravages of totalitarian governments that gained and retained power by brutal conquest and oppression. Those 200 years represent a dramatic inflection in the history of Western Civilization—a period of rapid change and enormous leaps in quality of life that began during the Industrial Revolution and transformed Western Europe and the United States.

Herman Kahn, the great futurist and the founder of the Hudson Institute, called this upward inflection the beginning of the "Great Transition," a 400-year span during which nearly everyone in the world should go from relative poverty to prosperity and well-being. That first 200 years of increasing prosperity only represents about one day out of a U.S. person's life expectancy of about 30,000 days—compared to the 5,500 years of civilization. We are privileged to be living our "one day's worth" after that period.

A good indicator of prosperity and well-being—and, by extension, an indicator of our progress along Kahn's Great Transition—is per capita gross domestic product (GDP). GDP represents the total dollar value of all goods and services produced during a particular period.

The graph nearby shows per capita GDP for the past 1,000 years for China and Western Europe, and puts into perspective just how different life today is from, effectively, the entirety of human history. (The flat line from the year 1,000 to 1,800 would be just about as flat going back 50,000 years.)

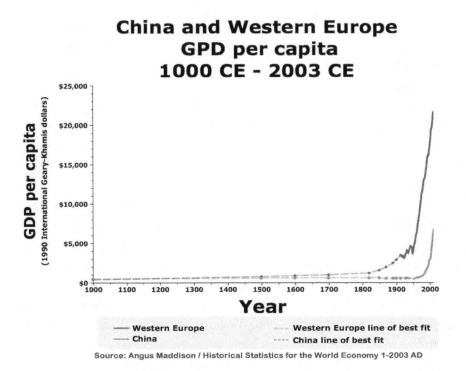

China and Western Europe
GPD per capita
1000 CE - 2003 CE

Source: Angus Maddison / Historical Statistics for the World Economy 1-2003 AD

If Kahn is right, then today we are more than halfway through his predicted transition—perhaps more, considering that his 400-year transition might be reduced to 300 years due to the information and communications revolutions which are propelled by Moore's Law and free people. In other words, if we don't screw things up, world populations could be only 80-100 years away from the general prosperity Kahn predicted.

There is a catch, however.

Our continued movement toward this prosperity isn't guaranteed. Note that on the GDP graph, life began to improve in Western Europe shortly after 1800, during the Industrial Revolution. The same phenomenon began around the same time in the United States. China, on the other hand, isolated itself from developments elsewhere in the world—the flow of civilization. Order was maintained by strong authoritarian governments. As a result, it took them about 150 years longer to reach their point of upward inflection. As we'll see, time and time again in the pages that follow, governmental and societal operating systems choices matter—a lot.

Today, we in the U.S.A. live in an exceptional country, during an exceptional time. In the context of human history, we enjoy freedoms and living standards far greater than at any time in the entire 100,000-year journey of the human species. It is a time when noble ideas about freedom, free enterprise, and new technologies create a bounty of opportunity for all people on earth.

That bounty, however, is not the result of random chance. To understand how our prosperity might continue, it is important that we first understand what drove Western Civilization's dramatic upswing in the first place—and why that upswing was so delayed, or failed to happen at all, in other regions.

It was energy that first put the Industrial Revolution in high gear. We developed new sources of power—burning wood and coal to boil water and to make steam—that enabled steam engines for boats, railroads and factories. But even more important than new sources of energy, the British Magna Carta in 1215 gave us new *ideas*. The decree emphasized the importance of the individual, and supported the idea that all people should be free to live and work as they pleased and have the benefits of their labors, including rights to their own property—rights that were ensured by the rule of law based on the Magna Carta.

As a free people with expanding knowledge and new sources of energy, we established governments relatively free of corruption. Coupled with mankind's inherent desire for improving life, these developments unleashed human productivity on a scale never seen before. That productivity phenomenon was multiplied further by dramatic improvements in scientific knowledge and innovation. That resulted in free people and free markets making new and better products more efficiently and less expensively.

And so, it was that for two centuries, freedom, free enterprise, and responsible government propelled Western Civilization upward through the first half of Kahn's transition to where we find ourselves today. Now, with two hundred years of hindsight, we can clearly see that with energy, responsible pluralistic governments, and free people working and innovating in free enterprise economies, there can be almost infinite improved living standards through wealth creation. Our own history tells us that the creation of higher living standards and wealth is not a zero-sum game.

We have also seen that socialist and communist countries have tended to trash the environment. The sense of ownership and responsibility inherent in property rights has extended to better environmental stewardship.

There is a singular lesson in the history of Western civilization's rise to prosperity: *choices of governmental and economic "operating systems" matter.* When bad decisions are made, it takes a long time to "reboot," and if the "hard drive" crashes, we can lose everything—in our case, our exceptional Constitution and rule of law. Protesters may bemoan our current culture and push for socialist principles that they believe will improve society, but the stunning advances that fuel Kahn's transition cannot be robust in a socialistic, authoritarian world.

With the right governmental operating system, all people can ultimately shed the yoke of poverty and authoritarianism. This book is an effort to remind us of the unique advantages of freedom and free enterprise, and why those values, rather than Marxist socialistic collectivism, should guide the world of the future through Kahn's "Great Transition" to prosperity for everyone.

INTRODUCTION

In the late 1950s, my brother Neal and I founded a banana *plantación* in Nicaragua. At the time, Central America was the closest thing to a "frontier" for a couple of motivated young men seeking to build their future. We spoke Spanish, had the mobility of being pilots, and after some legwork, both on the ground and in the air, we settled on Nicaragua as the best place to start the farm that would become our business.

By 1961, despite more than a few challenges, our banana enterprise seemed to be finding its footing, and we began to consider next steps. We reasoned that we could become more profitable by adding more value to our product at the source, and to that end, I bought a banana puree machine in the U.S., and made plans to fly it to our farm. There, we'd use it to make baby food, thus processing bananas ourselves and commanding a higher price, instead of selling them as a lower-priced commodity.

In March of 1961, I had the machine loaded on our twin-engine plane, and headed out. I made a fuel stop in Tampa, Florida and spent the night there, planning to fly to Key West the next day and then directly on to Nicaragua.

The week previous, I had been in Michigan exploring the possibility of selling banana puree from our farm to Gerber Baby Foods. While in Tampa, I ran into Donald L. Swenson, the Gerber executive I had met in Michigan.

Don was on his way to Mexico City on a business trip. I suggested instead that he accompany me to Nicaragua for the weekend, so he could see our banana farm in operation. After the weekend at the farm and a visit to Managua, I would put him on a commercial flight to Mexico City and he could continue his trip without missing a beat.

An adventurous guy, Don cancelled his flight and joined me. Spirits were high; we expected an uneventful journey and a pleasant weekend.

Neither of us had any idea what was in store for us.

At the time, I was flying a used 1950s Beechcraft Twin Bonanza business airplane. I knew the seven-seat Beechcraft had enough range to fly non-stop from the southern U.S. to Nicaragua if we followed a direct route. I filed an Instrument Flight Rules (IFR) flight plan on the international airway that would take us more or less directly to our destination.

Flying straight to Nicaragua from our planned fuel stop in Key West meant following an air corridor that passed almost directly over Havana, Cuba. The island runs east to west for some 600 miles, so the only other option would be to fly around it. That would have taken an extra fuel stop, and possibly another day.

The geographical and political situation was somewhat tense at the time, due to the stridency of the Castro regime and the strained relations between the U.S. and Cuba, but I didn't anticipate any trouble. International airways were established and well-used travel routes with prescribed standard procedures. We did everything by the book, filed our flight plan, and expected no issues.

The next day, with the rear of the plane loaded with equipment, and Don up front, we had a nice flight from Tampa down to Key West to fuel up. The border patrol inspected the airplane, ascertained that we had no contraband on board, and gave us their blessing to continue our trip. We left Key West, climbed to our proposed cruising altitude of 8,000 feet, and began the trip south.

Our flight along the international airway was uneventful until we approached Cuba. Clouds were building over the Cuban landmass, so I requested clearance to climb to 10,000 feet to get above them.

This should have been a routine approval but my request was met by radio silence. After an unusually long wait, the controller came back on the radio and said I was to proceed directly to Havana and land.

I responded that I would return to Key West instead. The controller countered that clearance back to the U.S. was denied, that I was to proceed directly to Havana, and that two jet fighters were being vectored to intercept us to make sure I complied.

I didn't have much time to think; any attempt at evasion could have resulted in our being shot down. It seemed there was little choice but to continue to Havana as ordered. I reasoned that the most likely outcome was for the Cubans to inspect the plane, find that we had no contraband on board, and let us go on our way.

I was sorely mistaken.

When we landed at the airport in Havana, we were immediately surrounded by machine-gun-toting *barbudos,* the bearded rebels who constituted the bulk of Fidel Castro's army. Looking out from the plane at the stern-faced rebels in military gear, it became apparent that our unplanned stop in Havana was not going to turn out as I expected.

The barbudos said we were to be taken to G2 (Intelligence) headquarters, where there would be an investigation of our flight. I was feeling a little apprehensive, but I still didn't believe we were really in danger. Although I was anxious to get on to Nicaragua, I optimistically thought we might at least see a bit of Havana and then be on our way.

The barbudos had other ideas.

G2 Headquarters was in central Havana, where the rebels had taken over a spacious villa in a vine-covered, upscale neighbourhood, and transformed it into an interrogation center and prison. There, Don and I were interrogated for about ten hours by two to three men, with a principal interrogator who conducted most of the questioning.

There were three things in the back of my mind during the interrogation. First, I had a handgun in my luggage. It was a simple and prudent measure for travel in Nicaragua, especially for dealing with the ever-present snakes on the *plantación,* but I thought the interrogators might attempt to make it into a something more than it was.

Second, I wondered if I still had a copy in my briefcase of a cover letter I had sent to U.S. Intelligence along with photos of a Cuban airbase in western Cuba that I had taken during a previous flight. I had taken the photos because I was concerned about what appeared to be a new military installation equipped with jets. At that time, we knew very little about what the Cubans were doing under Castro, and I thought the photos might be of military interest to the U.S.

Lastly, I had a pass with me to the Presidential compound in Nicaragua. Like the handgun, I was concerned that the intelligence operatives might read more into it than was justified.

I knew I couldn't do anything about the contents of my briefcase or the gun, but I did what I could: I tore up the presidential pass and put it down the toilet drain hole in the jail.

During the hours that followed, I told my interrogators about the banana puree machine, and answered what seemed to be an endless series of questions. they appeared to be satisfied with the explanation of the machine—I never heard anything more about it or the gun.

Our interrogation finally ended around 11 p.m. The rebels' report concluded with the phrase *muerte a los invasores,* or "death to the invaders," a phrase that was likely standard protocol for them, but didn't help my growing apprehension.

I was relieved that the interrogation had ended without physical duress, but the prospect of what might lie ahead made my stomach churn. I looked over at Don and knew he was feeling the same. The poor guy had been anticipating a tropical vacation weekend, and now he was being held in a foreign country with what felt like very uncertain prospects.

After removing us from the interrogation room, our jailers walked us down a hall and stopped at a wooden door. One of the men unlocked it and tugged it open, releasing a wave of damp, fetid air—the smell of many bodies in a small space. It wasn't until the light came on, however, that I could see there were nearly forty men crammed into a space about 14' x 19' with a high ceiling.

The men, all Cuban in appearance, filled the room. Some lay on double-decker bunks. Still others slept on the bare marble.

The guards slammed the door and left. We stared about the room, uncertain what to do until one man took charge and told the others to make room for us so we could lie down on the floor.

I would come to know this man as Gaspar Domingo Trueba Varona, the natural leader of the prisoners, and a natural leader of men.

One of the prisoners gave us a piece of paper to lie on. It wasn't much but it was better than the cold marble. The only way Don and I could both fit in the small space we were given was for me to slide halfway under one of the bunks; it was too low for me to slide completely under. When I needed to turn over, Don had to move aside so I could get out from under the bed, turn over, and then slide back under.

Sleep came grudgingly. About 3:00 a.m., the door opened, the lights came on, and they ordered Don and me outside. Not long after, we stood in front of a bank of high-intensity floodlights backed by television cameras. My heart sank; it was clear they were going to turn our "capture" into a news story.

The Cubans seemed determined to make a big deal out of something completely innocent. Though I was simply a young businessman, they accused me of being an invader. The questions continued, as we stared blindly into the wall of lights.

Finally, we were taken back to our cell, exhausted. We tried to catch a few winks before the sun came up.

As day broke, we could see more of our quarters. We were in one room of what had obviously been a comfortable, upscale home before it was taken over by the revolutionaries. Any sign of the fine décor that might once have been there was now gone, replaced with ten bunk beds for the forty people inside.

With no idea what might happen next, or when, or even *if* we'd be freed, we settled in to wait.

Slowly, anxiously, hours began to pass.

Then days.

———

We soon learned that sleeping arrangements in our cell were a matter of seniority. The captives who had been there longest had the best positions. The more recent arrivals, like Don and me, had the option of standing or lying on the marble floor. After a few days, we were considered sufficiently senior to merit bunk beds. When there was only one bunk, I insisted that Don take it. Eventually, I got one of my own.

We were fed twice a day, but only rice. Even now, decades later, I have a problem eating rice. The taste immediately takes me back to those harrowing days.

The room had a high window and was light during the day. There were overhead lights, but they were turned off around 10 pm. The time passed, but other than the change of day to night, there was no reliable way to mark the hours. After three or four days, I began to lose my sense of time.

Occasionally, guards would arrive, and remove prisoners. Some never returned. We could only speculate on what had become of them, and with each passing day, our own prospects became even more uncertain and disturbing. Every time the door opened, there was a sense of torturous anticipation. While I desperately wanted them to call my name in the hope of being released, I recognized they might just as easily be calling me to my execution.

In between those anxious moments, I thought endlessly about my situation and what was going to happen. We were constantly aware of the potential for being executed, although we clung to the hope that it wouldn't happen. I felt somewhat confident that because we hadn't done anything wrong, justice would eventually prevail and we'd be allowed to go free. That was naïve, but it helped me stay positive. Regardless, there was nothing we could do to influence the outcome. I simply had to focus on the possibility of being released.

Beyond that, there was little to do but wait, worry, and try to pass the time. I made a point of staying on my feet as much as I could, walking around in circles so I would not become physically debilitated. In American prisons, there's an exercise period where prisoners can go outside into the yard. There was nothing like that in the Cuban prison. There was no recreation other than walking in circles or doing pushups if you could find the space.

And so, I walked, I thought, and I hoped.

———

As happens to those in close quarters with nothing to do, we began to grow closer with the men in the room. Our fellow inmates were gracious and generous, and had obvious high regard for the United States. Since I spoke Spanish, I could communicate and get to know them, especially the leader Domingo Trueba. He spoke some English, but we conversed mostly in Spanish.

Domingo was an owner and operated a coffee company in lively late-1950s Havana. The size of a line-backer, with a rich, deep voice, he was a family man, with a wife and four children. He was about 34 when I met him, although he seemed older. Much was on his mind.

Domingo's company, Café Regil, prospered during the initial democratic reign of President Fulgencio Batista. When Batista declared himself dictator, Domingo became disenchanted and joined Fidel Castro's revolution in the Sierra Maestra mountains.

At first, Castro claimed his intention was to create a democratic free enterprise society. It wasn't long before his actual direction became evident, to the consternation of the many who thought they were following an enlightened and democratically-oriented leader. In 1960, Castro made it clear that he wanted to make Cuba a communist state. Che Guevara and others became Castro's communist sycophants, forcing their totalitarian ways on the populace. Domingo recognized Castro as a fraud who had no intention of implementing the promises he had declared for his revolution.

As the U.S. became alarmed at Castro's direction, the CIA began talks with the developing broad-based opposition to Castro. Domingo, his men, and others like them became the nucleus of forces hoping to overthrow the dictator. This new group of revolutionary fighters prepared to launch what was to become the Bay of Pigs invasion.

But Castro had developed a very effective counter-intelligence system as a part of his police state, and the insurrection plans were compromised. Domingo was arrested by Castro's forces and consigned to G-2 (intelligence) headquarters in Havana, along with many other counter-revolutionaries. Many of them had fought together in the Sierra Maestra on Castro's side before the movement turned to communism.

Now they languished in prison, labelled as traitors to the revolution.

Like Domingo, all the prisoners had stories to tell, but we were cautious in communicating. We knew there were informants in the cell, but we didn't know who they were. We kept our conversation light, although I was able to learn a bit about their hopes and aspirations for a free Cuba. One of the more memorable prisoners was Manuel Ñongo Puig. His wife was also incarcerated. He was more worried for her than for himself, but we were afraid to talk much about it. I learned later that he had been executed about 14 days after I was released.

I spent 9 days in that room. They were days spent with nothing to do, and nothing to read—time spent in a sort of strange, purgatorial mix of boredom and fear. About a week into our incarceration, the guards arrived and took Don from the cell. I had no idea where he was being taken, and that added an extra layer to my ever-present anxiety.

To pass the time and ease my mind, I played cards with the other prisoners, mostly Gin Rummy. I had never been very good at cards, but since there was nothing else to do, I worked at it. I even ended up winning a few games.

The Cubans were good, fun-loving men. They were making the most of a bad situation. Domingo and I formed a quartet with a couple of others, and from time to time, we entertained ourselves by singing, mostly in Spanish. They taught me Cuban songs and I taught them some Nicaraguan songs which I had learned during the previous years of developing the banana farm.

But through it all, the ever-present possibility of execution hung over our heads. As our friendship strengthened, and our future became increasingly less certain, I told Domingo, "If I ever get out of here, I will tell your story."

———

After nine days in that prison, the barbudos arrived without warning and ordered me out of the cell. They took me outside and threw me in a car between two armed guards. I had no idea if I was going to be shot or released.

To my surprise, they transferred me to the location where Don was being held. I was relieved to find him well, and cautiously hopeful when he told me we were going to be released and returned to the U.S.A.

The new facility was much nicer than the prison room, and featured the relative luxury of beds to sleep on. We weren't free to roam around, and they still only served us rice twice a day (although sometimes they added a little chicken broth), but all told, it was a far more comfortable existence.

When I was reunited with Don, he believed we were within a day of getting out. We would ask our guards what to expect, and sometimes we'd get an answer, but we could never be sure if the information was accurate. There was no way to tell if the people in this new jail really knew anything. We hoped it was true that we would be released, but we knew we couldn't count on it. We alternated between hope and despair. We had no control whatsoever over our own lives. Maybe we were going to live; maybe we were going to die.

Life in the Cuban prison was my first experience with how powerful it is to lose one's freedom.

After an additional three days, they drove us in a van, still sandwiched between guards, to the airport. There was a commercial Pan Am DC-6 on the ramp. To the right, on the tarmac, I could see our little private plane. It seemed an eternity since we'd first touched down.

When they began to march us toward the DC-6, I told them there was a mistake—our plane was over to the right. The barbudo guarding me shoved his machine gun in my back, and that was the last protest I made.

In a police state, you quickly learn it's best to keep your mouth shut.

As distressing as it was to leave our plane there on the ramp, I was glad to get out any way I could. Our flight to freedom was an unassuming, scheduled commercial flight. There were no military personnel or obvious diplomats on the plane, and the other travelers—all Cubans, as far as I could tell—seemed unsurprised to see two new passengers being led across the tarmac to the plane with guns in their backs. It wasn't an unusual sight in Cuba. Once we boarded the plane, no one said a word to us.

Although we were now sitting on what seemed to be a flight out of Cuba, the situation still seemed extremely precarious. I held my breath, unable to believe we were really getting out.

After what felt like a very long time, the doors closed—a good sign. When the engines finally started, I felt my heart beat faster. Then, at last, we taxied and took off to the south, then turned and headed north. That was another good sign, but I wasn't going to feel safe until we were over international waters.

As the Cuban coast passed below us, I allowed myself a little more optimism.

Finally, when I felt we were in international airspace, I released the biggest sigh of my life.

I was going to live and know freedom again.

———

It was some time before I learned the details of our release. The U.S. no longer had diplomatic relations with Cuba, but because Don Swenson was married to a Canadian woman, the Canadian Embassy had begun to work our case. Since Cuba had no quarrel with Canada, Don was to be released, which was why he'd been removed from our location early.

My situation was murkier. Unbeknownst to me, my parents had learned that I was in Cuba from the man who sold me gas in Key West. The border patrolman who had inspected our airplane told him the Cubans had reported my landing in Havana and cancelled my flight plan. Since my friend in Key West knew I had no intention of going to Cuba, he called my parents using the information on my credit card and gave them the news. My brother Neal got the news from the control tower in Managua, Nicaragua. He immediately began working for my release with Senator Gordon Allott of Colorado, a friend of our parents from college days at the University of Colorado.

Our parents' instinct was to keep my detention quiet and work behind the scenes to get me out. Meanwhile, another friend in Denver, Larry Ulrich, also heard about my confinement and contacted Colorado Senator Peter Dominick. Both Senators Allott and Dominick believed strongly that keeping quiet would probably mean I would simply disappear.

The Senators insisted that the U.S. should demand that the Cubans acknowledge I was there and state the charges against me. That became the new strategy, along with recruiting the help of a Canadian law professor named Maxwell Cohen, who was supposed to energize the Canadians to action.

I never did hear the full story of what happened, but apparently the Canadians and the Swiss Embassy, acting for the U.S. at the time, demanded that the Cubans admit we were there, and state the charges against us. Eventually, the pressure was enough to force our release.

———

By the time we reached Miami, reporters had heard the news and were in the airport waiting. It was the first time we had spoken to anyone as free men since we landed in Cuba nearly two weeks earlier. We answered their questions, endured the cameras, and finally, we left.

I was emotionally and physically exhausted, but I had a story to tell that went beyond superficial discussions with reporters, and so I headed for Washington, D.C. I coordinated my trip to Washington with Larry Ulrich and his boss Harry Combs, also of Denver. Harry, a great aviator and the owner of Combs Aircraft, was a Yale graduate, and one of my long-time mentors. One of his classmates was a man named Tracy Barnes, who was fairly high up in the CIA.

When Barnes heard about my Cuban experience, he asked Harry to get the three of us together for lunch at the Metropolitan Club in D.C.

During the extended lunch, I had the opportunity to tell Barnes everything I knew about my captivity.

As it turned out, this was all happening just days before the Bay of Pigs invasion. Naturally, Tracy was interested in anything going on inside Cuba. What he did, if anything, with my information, I don't know. I was only able to give details about the inside of the headquarters where I was held.

I imagine he found my description of Domingo Trueba interesting. I learned later that Domingo was to be their point man inside Cuba to lead an insurrection after the invasion. I don't know whether he was already aware that Domingo had been arrested; he revealed little of what he knew.

On April 17, 1961, less than two weeks after my release from Cuba, Cubans loyal to America landed at Playa Girón in what would become known around the world as the disastrous Bay of Pigs invasion.

The invasion party had trained in Guatemala, and from there, had moved to Puerto Cabezas in Nicaragua where they embarked for Cuba. I had seen some of the preparations in Puerto Cabezas, but the barbudos had never learned about that from my interrogation. Had they learned about the invasion coming from Nicaragua, that probably would have meant curtains for me.

I prayed the free Cuba forces would be successful in their mission, but it quickly became obvious it wasn't going that way. The invasion failed miserably and Castro cemented his hold on the Cuban people.

———

Though I was safe back in the U.S. I was plagued with worry for Domingo Trueba and the others I'd met in the Cuban prison. I made enquiries, and eventually heard through a friend with connections, that Domingo, Ñongo and others had been taken to *El Paredón* (The Wall) at La Cabaña prison. There, just a couple of days after the failed invasion, Domingo, Ñongo Puig and other companions faced a firing squad. Domingo's quest to bring freedom to his country was over. Ñongo's final words to his wife Ofelia were: "Don't worry Ofie. At least I know what I'm dying for." Fortunately for Ñongo's peace of mind, he could not have imagined the Castro regime of oppression and deprivation would last for sixty years . . . . and counting.

These were terrible blows. Friendship and connection are more a function of intensity than time, and being in the Cuban prison with Domingo was about as intense as you could get. Particularly with Domingo, I felt I had lost a very dear friend. He was a wonderful man and would have had a brilliant future ahead for him, his family and for Cuba. Unfortunately, that fabulous life force was cut short in its prime.

My time in the prison with Domingo is described in detail in a letter I wrote October 15, 1961 to Domingo's wife a few months after he was executed. The letter is reprinted in the Appendix beginning on page 168.

As it turned out, The Bay of Pigs invasion and the U.S. behavior there emboldened Khrushchev and precipitated the Cuban Missile Crisis about a year and a half later. It was an event that took the world closer to nuclear Armageddon than ever before or since.

A great power is usually criticized when it appears aggressive. It is despised when it appears weak. By being party to the invasion, the U.S. appeared aggressive. By withdrawing critical support that doomed the invasion, the U.S. appeared weak.

Eighteen months later President Kennedy responded with strength in the Cuban missile crisis, sending an armada of ships to stop the Soviet ships bearing more nuclear weapons and ballistic missiles, and Armageddon was avoided. But the Cuban people have since been consigned to more than a half-century of subjugation during a time when most of the world has made huge progress in living standards.

———

I believe freedom represents a fundamental human yearning. Those who have never experienced it believe it may be impossible or out of reach. Those who have lost it want it back. All too often, however, those who live with freedom tend to take it for granted.

It is very difficult to relive my experience. But I am intensely interested in extending the cause of freedom, particularly for those subjected to tyranny in Cuba, and the many who have lost their lives resisting it. If I do nothing else with this book but give people an understanding of life under tyrannical rulers, I will feel gratified.

Deep within a Cuban prison, I learned a great lesson about the value and blessing of freedom, and how easily it can be stripped away. It is my promise to Domingo to tell his story that prompted me to begin this book, but what drove me to complete it goes far beyond one man. This book is an effort to remind us all of the unique advantages of freedom and free enterprise, and why those values, rather than Marxist socialistic collectivism, should guide the world of the future.

In the pages that follow, I set forth the historical bases for our ideals of freedom, and give concrete examples of the tragic fall of those countries whose leaders misled their citizens with false hopes of a socialist utopia. It is my hope to amplify on the ideas that make for free people and the free market systems and why they are the best answers to poverty and social injustice.

Linden Blue

San Diego, California

1

FREEDOM OR SOCIALISM?

Why you can't have both, and
what drives the uninformed attraction to socialism

The problem with socialism
is that eventually you run out
of other people's money.

- Margaret Thatcher, former Prime Minister of England

The fundamental purpose of this book is to look seriously at whether we should base our future on the ideas of freedom or socialism—what works and what does not work for human progress and improvement of the human condition.

We started with the historical context; what life has been like through most of history. In 1651 Thomas Hobbes described it as "solitary, poor, nasty, brutal and short." Reality says that much of history has been replete with conquests, destruction, oppression, brutality and misery. Having defenses and deterring adversaries has been essential. The cost of losing in battles has frequently meant death, loss of family, subservience, slavery and serfdom.

The long evolution of civilization has included better ways, better ideas, better "operating systems" for people getting along and working constructively in a world of seemingly limited resources and opportunities. Assuring civil behavior hasn't been easy. Tribes, city states, nations, even families have been known to fight each other. Our founders were driven by the quest for the best ways of governance to assure civil adjustments of differences, minimize violence, and to make a republic last. They had felt the injustices of rule from afar by the sometimes arbitrary and greedy whims of a powerful monarch. In their decision for revolution they risked everything—their homes, their assets, their sacred honor and their lives.

Because of their foresight, courage and sacrifice, we can now look forward to a world of unlimited knowledge, resources and increased human productivity. Their revolutionary ideas laid the foundation for improvement of the human condition everywhere. Herman Kahn envisioned that this kind of progress would make the great four-hundred-year transition happen.

Others in search of better ways have been seduced by the utopian ideas of Karl Marx and Friedrich Engels. They were focused on the restraint of free market capitalism and the distribution of wealth rather than its creation. Inevitably, taking away the fruits of one's labor and giving it to others requires force—political, economic and putative. It means government by coercion rather than consent. It means control by political elites rather than individual responsibility and autonomy. It comes at a cost to our freedom, progress, and prosperity.

A time-honored way to get political support is by promising people free stuff. The problem is, free stuff must first be produced by someone before it can be given to someone else. Robbing Peter to pay Paul can work politically. It usually assures the political support and subservience of Paul. That is what makes socialism function. It is the foundation of socialism's "operating system."

To understand the high stakes of selecting socialistic ideas, we must begin by examining the notion that we can have it both ways.

We must fully realize that inherent in a choice of socialism as a system of government, is yet another choice. It is one in which we sacrifice our freedoms.

My experience in a communist Cuban prison led me to value freedom more than ever before. In the more than fifty years since I was freed, I have never forgotten what it felt like to lose my freedom. It was the most demeaning, demoralizing, frightening, suffocating experience of my life—it haunts me to this day. While I regained my freedom, the disaster for the Cuban people had only just begun. They stand as a perfect example of the incompatibility of socialism and liberty.

Many people, particularly those in the West, take their freedom for granted because they have never lost it. They wake up in a home or apartment. They have electricity, food, shelter, heat, potable running water and sanitation facilities. They can buy a car or a cell phone. They can shop freely, surrounded by abundance, without a second thought. They go about their lives without fear of arbitrary arrest.

At no time does it occur to them to think that the way they are living could be yanked out from under them without recourse. . . as it was for Domingo and his family.

These 'ordinary' aspects of life that we in the West take for granted share a unique quality: they can only be reliably enjoyed in a free society. The homes, the infrastructure that makes life comfortable and efficient, the cars, the movies, the meals—they are a product of a system that allows and rewards free speech, free enterprise, and free ideas. If you look to the failed socialist nations that litter history, few if any provided real hope for their people. Although nearly all came to power based on utopian slogans, they failed to provide a sustainable, prosperous way of life for their citizens.

This leads us to a paradox. Despite the dismal track record of socialist societies—one that we'll explore more deeply in coming chapters—there still exists an outspoken cohort that cries out for a further shift to socialist policies. For all the evidence that socialism is a failed system of government, there is a growing movement toward it.

Our journey begins with understanding *why*.

I believe that many people who say they support socialism do so because a) they lack real insight into socialist principles and actual socialist track records, and; b) because they have been convinced by outside sources that such principles are a benign way to provide "compassionate" government services that they believe will help society. As a result, they've fallen for the "have it both ways" trap, with little understanding of socialism or its consequences.

In the following pages, we'll look at what has created this misunderstanding, and work to clarify the real *modus operandi* of socialism, and the inevitable result of its application.

Millennials and the "More Generous Safety Net"

In October 2014, an interviewer questioned various attendees of a Congressional Caucus Conference and asked them to define socialism. No one interviewed was able to give a concise definition, and some seemed quite confused by the question. But almost without exception, the responders felt that a socialist is "someone who helps other people."[1]

For many, socialism seems a romantic concept. And if you only read the sales pitch, it sounds pretty good: no more class system, equality for all. The problem is that it rarely, if ever, works out that way. The only equality socialism truly offers is equality in poverty. The lofty claims of charismatic politicians are simply sugar-coated words that have rarely produced permanent positive results anywhere in the world.

According to Peggy Noonan of the Wall Street Journal, millennials, in particular, believe socialism is a "more generous social safety net."[2] They think of it as a harmless way to help the poor and downtrodden, create racial equality, and spread fairness. In their belief that socialism can accomplish these lofty ideals, they attend (sometimes violent) protests, give fiery speeches at events, and get themselves photographed with all the right people, hoping to further their cause.

---

1 http://www.thefederalistpapers.org/us/attendees-of-the-congressional-black-caucus-conference-asked-if-obama-is-a-socialist-also-whats-a-socialist. Accessed 7/18/15.

2 http://thefederalist.com/2016/02/15/why-so-many-millennials-are-socialists/. Accessed 2/15/16.

What they fail to see is the dark side of its pursuit—the inevitable loss of freedom that attends it, and the loss of prosperity that follows.

Millennials often declare themselves against capitalism. As Noonan points out, they have had a very different experience with capitalism than their parents and grandparents. Millennials have not seen the building of a nation through free enterprise, based on a governmental structure erected by our founders and expressed in the Declaration of Independence, the Constitution and the Bill of Rights. They did not experience the growth of wealth for all Americans that accelerated after the Second World War. They have not followed the progress of nations with an entrepreneurial spirit, whose governments allowed free-market capitalism to flourish, to the benefit of all.

Rather, they believe it was free market capitalism that "drove us into a ditch" in the 2008 U.S. recession. Their choice would have been "progressive" policies of excessive regulation and high taxes. The recession "shattered their faith in the system: its fairness, usefulness and efficacy."[3]

Millennials, it seems, are looking for something "new," something they believe will be more "fair." And many of them believe socialism would do the trick.

Why do they believe that?

It isn't because of wonderful socialist societies around the world; these are mostly imaginary.[4]

It isn't because they have studied economics and find that socialist principles help people; in the long run, they don't.

It isn't because socialist societies have made people happier and better off; their record on these issues is dismal.

Libertarian John Stossel wonders why young people don't see that socialism is not a good thing and has only made people *poorer* in the

---

3 Peggy Noonan. "Socialism Gets a Second Life." WSJ, 1/30-31/16. At A11.

4 For those who offer Sweden as an ideal socialist society, please see the section on Sweden.

countries where it has been tried,[5] including much of Central and South America.

One argument is that millennials haven't been given a chance to learn about free enterprise because most college professors are left-leaning and anti-business. As Noonan asks, who would have taught our youth about the wonders of the free enterprise system, or free trade, or the benefits of low taxes? Certainly not their teachers.

Noted economist Dr. Thomas Sowell might agree. He once said, "Socialism, in general, has a record of failure so blatant that only an intellectual could ignore or evade it."[6] Sowell was using the term "intellectual" to denote people who mainly think in the realm of theoretical possibility, not practical reality.

Unfortunately, this is the rule rather than the exception in most universities today. With such thinking, they reach conclusions that are devoid of the common sense and judgment that come from real-world experience. Instead, their "dumbed-down education is far more likely to offer the inspiring rhetoric of socialism than to present its dismal track record" in reality.[7]

And that's what socialism is: an abundance of rhetoric, paired with a scarcity of positive results.

Millennials don't seem to realize the tremendous benefits of the free enterprise system, even though they benefit from it. The high-paying tech jobs available on the market didn't come from government creation or control. They were created by entrepreneurs who, through the free

---

5 *Stossel.* 2/16/16. Fox Business Channel.

6 The renowned playwright, David Mamet, calls Dr. Sowell "our greatest contemporary philosopher." "Why I Am No Longer a Brain-Dead Liberal." March 11, 2008. http://www.villagevoice.com/news/david-mamet-why-i-am-no-longer-a-brain-dead-liberal-6429407. Accessed 2/17/15.

7 Thomas Sowell. "The Lure of Socialism." Townhall magazine. 2/17/16. http://townhall.com/columnists/thomassowell/2016/02/17/the-lure-of-socialism-n2120485. Accessed 2/18/16. Socialists manage to distance themselves from their failures, and when questioned on it, declare "That was never true socialism." https://fee.org/articles/why-socialism-is-the-failed-idea-that-never-dies/?fbclid=IwAR1rrWGc_g2ua2Cotz JTZV6n78aioAk_wrm2VrZ6 PmUCE15NCkTS9Hl6JqQ. Accessed 9/22/19.

market, were able to realize their innovative dreams, provide jobs for others, and change the world forever.

Bill Gates has said that he thinks socialism would help the world, but if he had tried to create his billion-dollar business under socialism, there probably would *be* no billion-dollar business nor all the increases in productivity that business has made possible. It's unlikely there would have been such rapid advancement of computers, and we would have fewer productive computer applications. There would be less advancement in the technical world, and a limited marketplace of ideas and supplies.

For millennials, adopting socialism may be a form of "rebellion." They don't want to follow the ways of their parents and grandparents. They want a system that they feel more closely relates to them. Something "new and exciting."

So, what do they want?

They appear to want high paying jobs that aren't too confining, an abundance of high-tech products, cool cars, and, of course, the ever-present smartphone. They especially want freedom in choosing their lifestyle.

For anyone who has studied history, it is mind-boggling that millennials think a socialist society will give them what they dream of. Socialism *takes away* individual freedom. Socialism controls what people do and say, and there is little innovation because it is not rewarded. There is limited production and there are fewer ground-breaking products to satisfy the wants and needs of the populace.

The Rise of Democratic Socialism

Millennials are not the only ones—this is not simply a product of youthful idealism. The tragic belief that socialism is a viable system of government has crossed all the demographic lines.

In 2015, during the 2016 U.S. election cycle, an interviewer from the Fox Business channel went to Greenwich Village in New York City and asked passersby whether they supported Socialism and Bernie Sanders, the socialistic candidate for President. An astonishing number said yes.

My guess is that if they were asked to define socialism, the response would have been silence.

It is mind-boggling that so many people profess support not only for a philosophy about which they know very little, but one that is guaranteed to progressively diminish personal freedoms. If you ask people who espouse socialist views to name a successful socialistic society, they tend to stammer. They say, like Bernie Sanders, "This is different. This is democratic socialism."

Nonsense. Socialism is basically an elitist approach to force people to do things the way government wants them done. There's no such thing as "democratic" socialism.

"Take from the rich, give to the poor," and "We will get rid of income inequality," are not new ideas. They are tired, age-old concepts that have been promulgated and dragged through generations by those who seek power, but fail to deliver the promised results.

On the MSNBC political show, *Hardball*, liberal host Chris Matthews asked former Democratic Party Chairwoman, Debbie Wasserman-Shultz, to define the difference between a Democrat and a Socialist. She had no answer.[8] She was the Chairperson of her Party, and could not differentiate Democrats from Socialists.

The reason? Socialists have had such a strong influence on the Democratic Party because most of their ideas and goals are very similar.

In 2016, the Democratic Party adopted almost every aspect of Bernie Sanders' Socialist platform, despite the lack of factual evidence that socialism builds strong economies. We might note here that in spite of espousing Socialism, Sanders himself owns three homes and drives an expensive car.

---

8 http://www.realclearpolitics.com/video/2015/07/30/chris_matthews_to_debbie_wasserman_schultz_whats_the_difference_between_a_democrat_and_a_socialist.html#!. Accessed 2/22/16.

The Hollywood Fantasy

In addition to our schools and left-leaning politicians, the influential world of Hollywood tends to be politically liberal, furthering the mistaken notion that socialism is a kinder, more generous form of democracy.

A paradox, as Milton Friedman puts it, in that "[m]any of those who profess the most individualistic objectives support collectivist[9] means without recognizing the contradiction."[10]

In their work and disciplines, creative people demand the utmost liberty and squawk endlessly if anyone interferes with their projects. They sometimes have a very hard time separating truth from reality. In their professional lives, they live in fantasy and they believe their own hype. Just because they say it, they believe it's the truth.

And yet in a fully totalitarian society, art forms are censored to the extent the government wishes. Artists are impeded from practicing their art in an individual way, forced instead into what the government approves.

Soviet Russia, for example, censored the arts and called the shots in artistic careers. The communists professed to be grand patrons of the arts, yet in Soviet Russia ballerinas were severely chastised if they went against what their communist bosses dictated for their professional careers. Two of the greatest dancers of the 20th century, Rudolf Nureyev and Mikhail Baryshnikov, defected to the West to control their careers because in the Soviet Union they were forced to follow the dictates of their totalitarian masters.

Isn't it paradoxical, then, that so many who consider themselves "creatives," are in large number supporters of socialist collectivist principles?

Similar to their socialist cousins, the Nazis censored art at their discretion. They banned modern styles as degenerate but promoted "traditional" art styles that reflected racial purity, militarism, and obedience.

---

9 Collectivist: Any philosophic, political, religious, economic or social outlook that emphasizes the interdependence of all people, as opposed to individualism.

10 F.A. Hayek, *The Road to Serfdom*. Chicago: U. of Chicago Press, 1994. At xi, Quoting from Friedman's 1971 introduction to the German edition of *The Road to Serfdom*.

They rejected jazz influences in music, and censored books, film, and theater.[11]

The Nazis burned the books of noted deaf and blind activist Helen Keller. In response, she commented, "Tyranny cannot defeat the power of ideas."[12]

The practice of censure also applied to the sciences. In communist Russia, a scientific discovery that did not conform to communist principles was discarded; science theory that was in accord was mandated.[13] [14]

David Mamet, the acclaimed playwright and a "reformed liberal" who converted to conservative politics, observes that when liberals ask you what your views are, they really aren't interested in what your views are. What they are trying to find out is if you are one of their "tribe," someone who believes as they do. If not, you are discredited and no further discussion ensues.[15]

We have seen that kind of environment increase since 2016, where the first amendment is under attack, freedom of speech is questioned, and the leftwing media fervently propels false news according to their liberal agenda. Even Howard Stern, the controversial radio "shock jock," has vowed that he will never vote for a Democrat again, saying "[T]hey're communists….It's gangsterism."[16]

Mamet also comments on the fact that no system is perfect.

> "The question is which of two systems is better able to discard the failed and experiment to find the new; and the answer is the Free Market. It is not perfect; it is *better*

---

11 http://www.historylearningsite.co.uk/censorship_in_nazi_germany.htm. Accessed 9/9/14.

12 http://www.ushmm.org/outreach/en/article.php?ModuleId=10007677. Accessed 9/8/14.

13 *See, e.g.,* Trofim Denisovich Lysenko, who embodied Marxist orthodoxy: Scientific dissent from his theories was formally outlawed in Russia in 1948. *See* J. Huxley, *Heredity: East and West* (1949), repr. 1969); Z. A. Medvedev, *The Rise and Fall of T. D. Lysenko* (tr. 1969); D. Joravsky, *The Lysenko Affair* (1970); V. N. Soyfer, *Lysenko and the Tragedy of Soviet Science* (1994).

14 http://www.britannica.com/EBchecked/topic/353099/Trofim-Denisovich-Lysenko. Accessed 9/9/14.

15 David Mamet, *The Secret Knowledge.* New York: Sentinel/Penguin Publishing Group USA, 2011.

16 https://www.youtube.com/watch?v=GwU_-Gek34I&sns=em. Accessed 9/8/15.

than State Control; for the Free Market, to a greater extent, must respond quickly and effectively to dissatisfaction and to demand – if a product or service does not please, to continue in its manufacture in the Free Market is pointless."[17]

What should be highly valued is "brainpower," enhanced and tempered by experience and judgment This is what produces environments that maintain freedom and prosperity in a market economy.

How Socialism Leads to Loss of Freedom

What the supporters of socialism fail to understand, despite the repeated lessons of history, is that socialism is not a state of effective governance, but the entry point to a path that leads inevitably to the loss of freedom.

The socialist platform, whether stated outright or not, is government ownership of the means of production. The rub is that by controlling the means of production, you control people's incomes, potential for asset accumulation and career choice. That means the redistribution of wealth rather than the creation of wealth. When the government controls and limits what individuals can keep, there is a disincentive to be productive and a fundamental limit to individual freedom—that in turn leads to fewer jobs created, and fewer occupational choices for individuals.

As incentives decrease, society as a whole becomes less productive and there is less wealth to share. This usually leads to totalitarianism, for as wealth declines, people must be *forced* to give up what they have worked for, rather than doing it willingly. The end result is government by force rather than government by consent—a society that, by definition, is not free.

As Dr. Thomas Sowell explains: "The real motives of liberals have nothing to do with the welfare of other people. Instead, they have two

---

17   Interview: David Mamet's Conservative Conversion, Uncommon Knowledge with Peter Robinson, The Hoover Institute, 11/22/2013.

related goals: to establish themselves as morally and intellectually superior to the rather distasteful population of common people, and to gather as much power as possible to tell those distasteful common people how they must live their lives."[18]

While socialism's stated high-minded purpose would be to enrich everyone equally, the result is that it impoverishes everyone except the politicians and bureaucrats who control government. Ultimately, those people serve their own interests and ideas, rather than the interest and ideas of individuals.

When former president Barack Obama was a community organizer, the handbook he used as a teaching tool was, "Rules for Radicals," by the infamous communist instigator Saul Alinsky.

Alinsky outlined the ways to bring down a capitalistic country, and turn it socialist. It is clear that Alinsky's professed goal was to have power *over* the people, not gain power *for* the people. That is usually the goal of socialism/communism: to have power and control in the hands of an elite few.

Alinsky's 13 Rules for Destroying a Capitalist Society:

1. "Power is not only what you have, but what the enemy thinks you have." Power is derived from 2 main sources — money and people. "Have-Nots" must build power from flesh and blood.

---

18 Dr. Ileana Johnson Paugh, quoting Dr. Thomas Sowell. "'Free Education With Strings Attached." 1/15/15. http://canadafreepress.com/article/69000. Accessed 8/30/15.

2. "Never go outside the expertise of your people." It results in confusion, fear and retreat. Feeling secure adds to the backbone of anyone.

3. "Whenever possible, go outside the expertise of the enemy." Look for ways to increase insecurity, anxiety and uncertainty.

4. "Make the enemy live up to its own book of rules." If the rule is that every letter gets a reply, send 30,000 letters. You can kill them with this because no one can possibly obey all of their own rules.

5. "Ridicule is man's most potent weapon." There is no defense. It's irrational. It's infuriating. It also works as a key pressure point to force the enemy into concessions.

6. "A good tactic is one your people enjoy." They'll keep doing it without urging and come back to do more. They're doing their thing, and will even suggest better ways.

7. "A tactic that drags on too long becomes a drag." Don't become old news.

8. "Keep the pressure on. Never let up." Keep trying new things to keep the opposition off balance. As the opposition masters one approach, hit them from the flank with something new.

9. "The threat is usually more terrifying than the thing itself." Imagination and ego can dream up many more consequences than any activist.

10. "The major premise for tactics is the development of operations that will maintain a constant pressure upon the opposition." It is this unceasing pressure that results in the reactions from the opposition that are essential for the success of the campaign.

11. "If you push a negative hard enough, it will push through and become a positive." Violence from the other side can win the public to your side because the public sympathizes with the underdog.

12. "The price of a successful attack is a constructive alternative." Never let the enemy score points because you're caught without a solution to the problem.

13. "Pick the target, freeze it, personalize it, and polarize it." Cut off the support network and isolate the target from sympathy. Go after people and not institutions; people hurt faster than institutions.[19]

---

19 http://www.openculture.com/2017/02/13-rules-for-radicals.html. Accessed 9/18/19.

"Rules for Radicals" are the tactics of tyrants. They pit people against each other. They are antithetical to the system of pluralistic sharing of responsibility our Founders framed. Our "Republic" provided an operating system where people could work together under constituted authority and justice in law.

The Slow Drift Away From Freedom

Part of our apparent inability to identify the dangers of socialism is the pace of its changes. Gaining power over people can be deceptively slow, accomplished through more and more legislation that gives government increasing power and control. It can happen almost beneath the level of perception, through decades, until a society suddenly realizes that the country has been stealthily transformed.[20]

We saw the drift to the left accelerate during the Obama administration. Obamacare is an example of the government making your decisions for you. Instead of doctors controlling your health decisions, the government regulators do so. There are even provisions for the so-called "Death Panels," when government regulators decide how much healthcare an elderly individual should receive.[21]

During the 2008 presidential campaign, President Obama was famously heard to say to a woman with a seriously ill mother, that her mother wouldn't be allowed to suffer pain: they would give her a pill. In other words, no surgery or other expensive treatments. Just a pain pill.[22]

That is socialism in action. President Trump vowed to repeal and replace Obamacare. He has been unable to get that done. All 48 Democrat Senators and 3 Republican Senators voted against him. Forty-nine Republicans voted to support him and replace Obamacare, but that wasn't enough.

---

20 "The Socialist Party will no longer be running a candidate for president. The Democratic Party is leading this country to Socialism much faster than we could ever hope to." Norman Thomas, 1944. Thomas was a Socialist candidate for U.S. President.

21 It is already starting. In 2017, the State of Oregon voted to allow dementia patients to be starved to death. https://www.lifesitenews.com/news/oregon-senate-passes-bill-allowing-dementia-mentally-ill-patients-to-be-sta. Accessed 8/28/19.

22 This incident even gave rise to a song, "We the People," by Ray Stevens:
"It's gonna be a big heart breaker.
Grandma needs a new pacemaker.
And the doctor says, 'I realize she's ill,
But there's talk of legislation, on all our medication,
And maybe all we can do is put her on a pain pill." -- Clyde Records (Nashville), 2012.

President Trump has repealed the individual mandate (requiring *everyone* to buy insurance whether they want to or not), expanded short term coverage, and reduced premiums.

A health care system that would rely on individual care and responsibility and free up medical practitioners would save everyone a lot of money.

Let the private market do its job, and many better and more economical alternatives will appear, as they did so for many years before Obamacare.

In *The New Road to Serfdom*, British delegate to the European Parliament, Daniel Hannan, enumerates the qualities of a free society: "Personal liberty, free contract, jury trials, uncensored newspapers, regular elections, habeas corpus, open competition, secure property, religious pluralism." Demonstrating the shift away from those things, he summarizes, "As the U.S. moves toward European-style health care, day care, college education, carbon taxes, foreign policy and spending levels, so it becomes less prosperous, less confident and less free."

Jonathan Chait, commentator and writer for New York magazine, explains the failure inherent in socialism:

"The reason every Marxist government in the history of the world turned massively repressive is not because they all had the misfortune of being hijacked by murderous thugs. It's that the ideology itself prioritizes class justice over individual rights and makes no allowance for legitimate disagreement."[23]

At present in the U.S. governments, federal, state and local control almost half of the American economy, says John Stossel, the Libertarian former talk show host. That's not the way to higher productivity and higher living standards. At the end of 2019, U.S. debt exceeded $23 trillion – an astonishing sum that equates to about $190,000 for each household. At that point, says Romina Boccia, a "geeky budget analyst from the Heritage Foundation," we will be paying more for interest on debt than we spend on the military and other federal priorities.

23 Kevin D. Williamson. "The Mugging Continues." 11/12/15. http://www.nationalreview.com/corner/426966/mugging-continues-kevin-d-williamson. Accessed 2/29/16; https://www.nationalreview.com/corner/morals-and-moralizing-yale-mario-loyola/. Accessed 9/21/19.

Political, religious, and cultural commentator Rev. Sirico also points to the drift inherent in socialism, saying, "Where a socialist organization of economic life has held sway, the result has not been the rise of social cooperation but its opposite – the decline of civil society and an increase in alienation."[24]

Perhaps, though, it was former Sheriff Joe Arpaio of Maricopa County, AZ, who said it best:

> "A liberal paradise would be a place where
> everybody has guaranteed employment,
> free comprehensive healthcare, free education,
> free food, free housing, free clothing, free utilities,
> and only law enforcement has guns.
> And believe it or not, such a place does, indeed, exist.
> It's called Prison."

There is No "Both"

The Oxford Dictionary defines freedom as: "The power or right to act, think or speak as one wants, without hindrance or restraint."

The Oxford Dictionary defines Socialism as: "A political and economic theory of social organization that advocates that the means of production, distribution, and exchange should be owned or regulated by the community as a whole."

Even this cursory analysis from the dictionary reveals an undeniable truth: Freedom and socialism are mutually exclusive. You cannot have both.

Under socialism, the "community" (read: authoritarian government) is actually a group of elite politicians who have convinced the public that they know better than the public how to run their lives. Because they know better, they convince the public that their policies and rules must govern.

They subsequently enact policies and rules that take away the freedom of individuals to act, think or speak as they wish, purportedly for the

---

24 Sirico. Rev. Robert A. *Defending the Free Market*. Washington, D.C.: Regnery Publishing, 2012.

good of the world. In actual practice, it's for the good of the leftist elite politicians. When proponents speak of the need for Global Government, they are promoting worldwide socialism, where an elite group of politicians would rule the world.

Karl Marx, author of the foundation document of communism, *Das Kapital,* viewed socialism as the transitional phase between capitalism and full-blown economic and social communism. When accused of "conflating" socialism with communism, economist Friedrich Hayek responded that it is not possible to conflate synonyms.[25]

As Vladimir Lenin, the murderous former ruler of Russia, said: "The goal of socialism is communism."

The World Socialism website[26] defines socialism in part as follows:

"Central to the meaning of socialism is common ownership. This means the resources of the world being owned in common by the entire global population.…. In practice, common ownership will mean everybody having the right to participate in decisions on how global resources will be used. It means nobody being able to take personal control of resources, beyond their own personal possessions."

"…everybody having the right to participate in decisions on how global resources will be used."

How would you ensure that everybody in a city or country would participate, or that they would agree? When you take a populace at large, there is no way to successfully control them centrally, unless you do so by force. That means you must either imprison dissidents or, as has been the case in Cuba and other totalitarian states, kill them. It turns out individuals really don't have a say in much of *anything.*

Here is an example of Marx's theoretical fantasies: Let everyone have their "fair share." It sounds good in theory. The problem is, it doesn't work in practice and has never worked anywhere in the world for a prolonged period. In fact, in his writings, Marx's ideas were almost entirely

---

25   Mike S. Adams. "My Apology to UNC-Charlotte." 11/13/07. http://www.distance-healer.com/html/democracy2.html. Accessed 10/7/15.

26   www.worldsocialism.org. Accessed 10/7/15.

theoretical. As Thomas Sowell asks, "What exactly is your 'fair share' of what someone else has worked for?"[27]

One economics professor points out that Marx's "predictions have not withstood the test of time. Although capitalist markets have changed over the past 150 years, competition has not devolved into monopoly,"[28] as Marx assured us it would.

Most people have participated in some way in a committee meeting or group project. How easy was it to get a consensus? How much compromise and discussion and argument ensued before a decision was reached? How many factions and cliques formed? How many different points of view were observed, how many heated exchanges?

It's not easy to make a group decision.

Yet, proponents of socialism promote "global ownership" where everyone is supposed to agree on what should be owned and in what proportion.

The concept is unworkable on its face. The massive project of trying to get everyone agreed on anything is next to impossible. What "global ownership" really means is that a government elite will make the decisions and dole out what they want, to whom they want, when they want, with the highest prizes going to the favored elite. Soviet Russia was a very good example; in their society, you only moved up if you were favored by the elite. Some say that Putin's Russia has much the same structure.

The official socialist site goes on to say that the ultimate result of following socialist principles would be that "everybody would have free access to the goods and services designed to directly meet their needs and there need be no system of payment for the work that each individual contributes to producing them. All work would be on a voluntary basis. Producing for needs means that people would engage in work that has a direct usefulness."

---

27 https://www.goodreads.com/quotes/679652-since-this-is-an-era-when-many-people-are-concerned. Accessed 9/21/19.

28 David L. Pritchitko, Economics professor at North Michigan University. "Marxism, an Appraisal." *The Concise Encyclopedia of Economics* . Indianapolis, IN: Liberty Fund, Inc. At 339.

Designed to directly meet their needs. In other words, we'll decide what you need.

No system of payment. In other words, you won't get paid for what you do or be able to determine what you receive for your labors.

Work that has a direct usefulness. In other words, the all-powerful State will decide what work you do and whether it is useful.

All work on a voluntary basis. In other words, lazy people won't work at all while others would have to work harder to make up for it.

It takes little imagination to conceive the ultimate result of such a policy: No free enterprise, limited social liberties, no financial independence, and no productive society. Look to Soviet Russia and Cuba in the 1960s, East Germany in the 1980s, and Argentina, Brazil, Cuba and Venezuela in the 2000s.

Since "all work" is voluntary, what if nobody wants to work? How many people do you know who would say, "I'm not doing anything. Let the State take care of me." What motivation is there to work hard? And without motivation what happens to productivity? It declines until the populace has very little access to a very small selection of goods, and an overall reduced standard of living.

"Free access" to goods and services doesn't mean much if goods and services aren't available—because no one has worked to produce them.

That was essentially the state of communist Soviet Russia toward the end of the 20th century. Anyone who worked for two years at *any* business was vested for life and could not be removed. Obviously, there were many who felt they didn't need to do anything since they got paid anyway, and Russia went steadily downhill until the whole system collapsed.

To say the people were "taken care of" in the Soviet Union is only minimally true. It was a miserly, miserable, unfulfilling existence, with a minimum subsistence level for all but the top government elite, and no prospect for the ordinary man or woman to change their lives. The communist state kept the people in ignorance because they were only allowed to view State TV and they knew little of the freedom and prosperity in other countries.

The same situation is present today in every country that has adopted socialism. Every country? Isn't that statement too categorical? Hasn't it worked well in Scandinavia? That is an important question. So important, I will devote most of Chapter 4 to it. The short answer here is that Scandinavian socialism probably isn't what you think it is.

No thoughtful person wants to see people without food, shelter, education, and at least a minimum of medical care. Remember, though, that any time the government provides a job, housing, welfare, health care, they control you. That's the whole idea—if they have control, they have power.

And therein lies the great deception of socialism. Proponents proclaim the ability to take care of the citizens as well or better than capitalism. But when businesses shut down because of suffocating regulation, where is the money that socialism depends on to give to the people? If you break the back of business, you cut off the supply of taxes necessary to support the expensive socialist/communist welfare programs.

Wikipedia has this to say: "In socialist economics the term [Socialism] usually refers to the process of structuring or restructuring the economy on a socialist basis, usually in reference to establishing a system of production for use in place of organizing production for private profit along with the *end of the operation of the laws of capitalism*." [Emphasis added.]

The State then controls everything and nobody can create a business or make a profit.

Marx "promises" that the socialist system will get rid of class prejudice and status and instead "we shall have an association, in which the free development of each is the condition for the free development of all."[29]

In other words, if I can't do what I want ("free development of each"), I'm not going to let you do what you want ("the condition for the free development of all").

---

29 Sirico, Rev. Robert A. *Defending the Free Market*. Washington, D.C.: Regnery Publishing, 2012. At 94.

"[N]obody being able to take personal control of resources…" means no free enterprise. Without profits, there is no incentive to form a private company that employs people, so there will be only businesses run by the inefficient government. Ludwig von Mises frames it this way: "'No one shall be idle if I have to work; no one shall be rich if I am poor.' Thus we see, again and again, that resentment lies behind all socialist ideas."[30]

Churchill was even more critical, condemning socialism as "a philosophy of failure, the creed of ignorance, and the gospel of envy. Its inherent virtue is the equal sharing of misery."

The "have nots" want what the "haves" have. And while there's nothing wrong with wanting to move up, when the only way to accomplish it is through subservience to the government, you have planted the seeds of decline. Socialism deprives people of opportunity. Only free enterprise capitalism provides the environment in which each participant can move up according to the degree of his desire, hard work, and innovation.

The problem is, most people have not studied history and do not understand what socialism really is. Keeping them in the dark is the main method used by despots who want to grab control.

The best evidence against socialism is its own track record—one that we'll explore in detail in the pages ahead. For now, suffice it to say that *no country in history has prospered for an extended period under socialism.*

Why?

Since socialism is a very inefficient producer, it is difficult to support the welfare state. Greece today is a good example of this. And there have been riots in the streets in Venezuela because the stores are out of food and the government is rationing gas and electricity. Libertarian John Stossel reports that military forces have to be stationed outside the stores to be sure that no one takes more than a certain amount of products.[31]

But what of the seeming success of some countries? It's a temporary condition, funded by resources provided earlier or elsewhere. For

---

30 Socialism: An Economic and Sociological Analysis. Carmel, IN: Liberty Fund/Liberty Classics, 1981. At 394.

31 *Stossel.* 2/16/16. Fox Business Channel.

the initial support of state socialism, for example, Soviet Russia had the treasury of the Czar. Sweden had built-up riches from their long period (almost one hundred years) of a pro-business economy. Communists in Cuba overthrew the previously prosperous government. Argentina arose out of the institutions of the Spanish Empire and had many natural resources. Venezuela had oil revenues. East Germany was initially funded by the Soviet Union.

When they turned to socialism/communism, each of these formerly prosperous countries descended into ruin.

Which brings us back to Margaret Thatcher's assertion that the problem with socialism is that eventually, you run out of other people's money.

Five basic truths which point out the basic flaws of socialism:

1. You cannot legislate the poor **into** prosperity by legislating the wealthy **out of** prosperity. When companies are legislated out of business, the taxes socialism counts on to provide its benefits go with them.

2. What one person receives **without working for**, another person **must work for** without receiving.

The Left is always talking about fairness. Dr. Thomas Sowell asks: "Why is it greed to want to keep the money you earn, but not greed to want to take somebody else's money?" Despots and elites have tended not to make that distinction.

3. The government **cannot give** to anybody anything that the government **does not first take** from somebody else.

Governments are political entities and live off of the taxes of working people and businesses. They have no other source of income (except in the rare cases where the government partners with a private entity). When a socialist government starts regulating heavily (placing heavier tax burdens on the people), many people stop working because it doesn't make sense to work when most of your money is taken by the government. Loss of working people and businesses means loss of taxes. Without the massive taxes, a socialist government cannot sustain its massive benefits programs and the system ultimately collapses.

This is why the Soviet Union (1917-1989) eventually fell into ruin. The same holds true with Venezuela, Argentina, Cuba—all societies under extreme stress.

4. You cannot **multiply** wealth by **dividing** it.

It is only by multiplying wealth (increasing the number of people who are successful and businesses that flourish) that a society continues to grow and prosper. When you take from those who earn, and give to those who don't earn, wealth (the general prosperity of a people) diminishes.

5. When half of the people get the idea that they **do not have to work** because the other half is going to **take care of them**; and when the other half gets the idea that it does

no good to work because somebody else is going to get what they work for, **that is the beginning of the end of any nation.** -- Adrian Rogers

Unfortunately, many of these ideas are prevalent in the Democratic party's ideological leadership in the person of sometimes Socialist Senator Bernie Sanders.

Socialism and the Assault on Free Speech

One of the sinister ways in which socialism takes over a culture is through repression of free speech. In his famous book, *1984*, about a totalitarian society gone mad, George Orwell illustrates what happens when the "Party" (the ruling elite) is in control:

"Every record has been destroyed or falsified, every book rewritten, every picture has been repainted, every statue and street building has been renamed, every date has been altered. And the process is continuing day by day and minute by minute. History has stopped. Nothing exists except an endless present in which the Party is always right."[32]

On the walls of the Reagan Library, in Simi Valley, California, is inscribed one of the sayings of the murderous Russian communist dictator, Josef Stalin: *"Ideas are more important than guns. We would not let our enemies have guns, why should we let them have ideas."*

And who are "the enemies"? Turns out it's anyone who doesn't agree with the despot.

Free speech was one of the cornerstones of the republic created by the Founding Fathers. Without free speech, all freedom is imperiled. It is a slippery slope; free speech is stripped a little at a time, while all the while a nation moves closer to a totalitarian state.

---

32 http://www.goodreads.com/quotes/481916-every-record-has-been-destroyed-or-falsified-every-book-rewritten. Accessed 7/18/15.

Most Americans believe in freedom and free speech, and yet commencement speakers with conservative views are being silenced and denied honorary degrees in colleges and universities across the country. Their opinions are deemed politically objectionable by academia. This has happened at American universities like Brandeis, Haverford, Rutgers, Smith, Swarthmore, Johns Hopkins, Berkeley, and others.

Mark Steyne points out that free speech is not a universal value. It arises from "a very narrow, particular tradition." He believes that as countries gain more Muslim residents, the concept of free speech will gradually disappear around the world. We are already seeing that happening in America. Crosses are being taken down because they might offend Muslims. People are afraid to say Merry Christmas for the same reason. And the list goes on.

Muslim immigrants who wish to enter the United States should be asked if they are comfortable with the U.S. Constitution, rather than Sharia law. If those who want to come into this country do not support our values and laws, why should we let them in? Especially if their publicly expressed view is to force their laws on us. Islam grew rapidly by offering those conquered the choice of converting to Islam, paying extra taxes, or being executed. These are not acceptable alternatives.

On many college campuses, the assault on free speech has become a vocation. One left-wing professor explained: "After the Vietnam War, a lot of us didn't just crawl back into our literary cubicles; we stepped into academic positions. With the war over, our visibility was lost, and it seemed for a while—to the unobservant—that we had disappeared. Now we have tenure, and the work of reshaping the universities has begun in earnest."[33]

This should concern all of us. As the Wall Street Journal said, "What was evident at the University of Missouri [2016 riots due to a shooting in Ferguson, MO], and in last weekend's confrontation over free speech at

---

33 "Every Crybaby Student Needs to See This One Meme About Safe Spaces." The Federalist Papers Project. 11/15/15. http://www.thefederalistpapers.org/us/every-crybaby-student-needs-to-see-this-one-meme-about-safe-spaces. Accessed 11/22/15.

Yale, is that political dialogue at universities is disintegrating to the level of 1968, when many schools became places of physical and intellectual chaos."[34]

Dr. Thomas Sowell notes that "...attempts to shut down people whose free speech interferes with other people's political agendas go on, with remarkably little notice, much less outrage. The Internal Revenue Service's targeting the tax-exempt status of conservative groups is just one of these attempts to fight political battles by shutting up the opposition, rather than answering them."[35]

One basic teaching of true liberalism [i.e., classical liberalism or conservatism/ libertarianism] is that the essential right of free people is the right to offend, and an essential responsibility of free people is to learn how to cope with being offended." [36]

Commentator George Will says never has freedom of speech been so "dangerously threatened" as it is now. It's an attack on "the *theory* of freedom of speech. It is an attack on the *desirability* of free speech and indeed if listened to carefully and plumbed fully, what we have today is an attack on the very *possibility* of free speech. The belief is that the First Amendment is a mistake. . . ."[37] [38]

In 2015, Ami Horowitz[39] visited the Yale University campus, testing whether Yale students would sign a petition advocating repeal of the First Amendment to the Constitution— the one that fundamentally guarantees freedom of speech. About 50% of the 100 students he talked to

---

34 http://www.siliconinvestor.com/readmsg.aspx?msgid=30312426; http://www.wsj.com/articles/bonfire-of-the-academy-1447200535?alg=y&mg=id-wsj. Accessed 11/12/15

35 "The New Inquisition." Realclearpolitics.com. 4/14/15. http://www.realclearpolitics.com/articles/2015/04/14/the_new_inquisition__126253.html. Accessed 11/7/15.

36 Stephens, Bret. The Wall Street Journal/Global View, "To the Class of 2014: Students who demand emotional pampering deserve intellectual derision." 5/19/14.

37 Debbie Young. "Attacking the Theory of Free Speech." 4/21/15. http://www.richardcyoung.com/essential-news/attacking-theory-freedom-speech/. Accessed 11/22/15.

38 "Free Speech has never been, in the history of our republic, more threatened than it is now." http://www.wsj.com/articles/notable-quotable-george-will-1429574911?alg=y&mg=id-wsj. Accessed 11/22/15.

39 https://www.youtube.com/watch?v=PknvApdz5e8. Accessed 2/5/16.

signed the petition. Apparently, the students are not aware that their right to protest is one of the activities guaranteed by the First Amendment.

George Will says we are raising a generation of kids who "believe they should have 'freedom *from* speech.'" That is a very dangerous trend.

Lately, even nuances have come under attack. We are not supposed to say someone is "working hard" because it will make someone who is not working hard feel bad. Likewise, we shouldn't call anyone exceptional.

Lies and the Cycles of History

It has been said that those who fail to study history, are doomed to repeat it.

When French historian and commentator Alexis de Tocqueville visited America in the 1800s, he came to observe democracy in action. In the end, he sought to dispel the notion that socialism and democracy are compatible. He put it this way:

> "Democracy and socialism have nothing in common
> but one word, equality. But notice the difference:
> while democracy seeks equality in liberty,
> socialism seeks equality in restraint and servitude."

I have spoken with many people who previously lived in repressive socialist/communist countries and now live in America. Without exception, they are amazed that Americans are falling for the very socialist propaganda that they came to America to escape.

The promoters of socialism in America have done a very good job. They have hidden de Tocqueville's "equality in restraint and servitude," and instead given it a pretty face. Most people respond well to a candidate who says he wants to help people, and sometimes that's all that's needed—nice words that lack substance but make a voter feel good.

The problem comes when people figure out they are the ones who have to pay the price through higher taxes. Of course, the politicians say they will only raise taxes on the wealthy, but, much to their surprise and chagrin, "the wealthy" ends up including the middle class. From there, socialists continue into over-regulation. Eventually, private businesses fail and all that remains is the government—one which has no idea how to promote growth or stimulate a successful, prosperous society.

Orwell wrote, "And if all others accepted the lie which the Party imposed—if all records told the same tale—then the lie passed into history and became truth. 'Who controls the past' ran the Party slogan, 'controls the future: who controls the present controls the past….'"

As Lenin said, a lie told often enough becomes the truth. Lies, sustained, are eventually accepted without challenge by young believers who see only the flaws in capitalism and don't acknowledge the benefits. The believers are swayed by charismatic liberal leaders who convince them that if they don't accept and support socialist principles, they are racists and elitists without compassion.

There has never been a more urgent time for truth. There is no common ground between socialism and freedom. The only citizens who benefit under socialism are the political elite—and as we'll see in the next chapter, the last 2,000 years provide us with a long track record of evidence.

During times of universal deceit,
telling the truth becomes a revolutionary act.

-- George Orwell

2

WHAT CICERO KNEW

Two thousand years of failed socialism

To be ignorant of what occurred before you were born is to remain always a child.
- Marcus Tullius Cicero

C hallenging the allure of socialist ideas isn't new. Marcus Tullius
Cicero,[40] whose letters from the first century B.C. are often credited
as one of the inspirations for the 14th century Renaissance, railed against
the concepts that one day would become known as socialism.

Nearly two thousand years ago, Cicero pointed out what we now
know from experience: when politicians touting social change speak of a
new or utopian society, they are often advocating what will turn out to
be a world ruled by dictators. The great orator's statements about Caesar
and the people of ancient Rome could just as well apply to America
today:

> "Do not blame Caesar, blame the people of Rome
> who have so enthusiastically acclaimed and adored him
> and rejoiced in their loss of freedom and danced in his path

---

40   A humble citizen of ancient Rome who worked his way up to Co-Consul of Rome in 63 b.c.
and was assassinated by agents of Caesar, who had been declared dictator for life in Rome (and was
himself assassinated months later).

and gave him triumphal processions. Blame the people
who hail him when he speaks in the Forum of the
'new, wonderful, good society' which shall now
be Rome's, interpreted to mean: more money,
more ease, more security, more living fatly
at the expense of the industrious."[41]

Cicero was more prescient than he knew

Our history since the fall of Rome is replete with examples of dictators
and despots who not only took their country's wealth under the banner
of socialism or communism,[42] but took the rights of their citizens with
it. As we'll see from the cases in this chapter, Cicero's statement that
"freedom is a possession of inestimable value" continues to hold to this
day.

Cry for Me, Argentina

At the beginning of the twentieth century, Argentina was one of the richest countries in the world. Blessed with abundant and verdant farmlands,
only the United States could equal its economic power.

That changed in 1916, when, in a pitch that may sound familiar
to Americans, a populist movement swept the *Unión Cívica Radical* ("The
Radicals") into power with a promise of fundamental change and an ap-
peal to the middle class.

The new president, Hipólito Irigoyen, began to implement a number
of socialist reforms, including mandatory pension insurance, mandatory
health insurance and support for low-income housing construction to

---

41 Quoted in 'Cicero's Prognosis" by Justice Millard F. Caldwell, *Presented at the 22nd Annual Meeting of the Association of American Physicians and Surgeons, Inc.*, October 7-9, 1965, Columbus, Ohio.

42 In this book, we use socialism and communism interchangeably, as one unavoidably leads to the other. "The goal of socialism is communism." Vladimir Lenin, founder of the Communist Party in Russia, 1912.

support the economy. As is often the case in socialist government, the State also assumed control of a huge section of the economy.

That control, however, came with new costs. The bureaucrats soon introduced a payroll tax and became overly generous with their entitlement programs. The money was spent faster than it could be collected, and soon the entitlements far outweighed the contributions of the citizens.

Enter Juan Peron and his charismatic wife, Eva Duarte, popularly known as Evita.[43] After helping to overthrow a weak civilian government, Peron remained part of the military regime until 1945, when, through the support of the labor unions and workers, he was elected President of Argentina with 56% of the popular vote.

Peron then instituted "The Third Position," an authoritarian and populist system between communism and capitalism, promising *justicialismo* (social justice), which included taxing the rich. The "rich," however, ended up including most of the middle class, which became an enemy to be targeted and humiliated by the government.

As the socialist machine expanded, state bureaucracies exploded and peasants from outlying farmlands flocked to the city to take advantage of lucrative state positions. The exodus of farmers created shortages in beef and wheat production, and after decades of being a major exporter of wheat, Argentina was forced to import.

Peron nationalized the railroads and utilities, and in some districts eliminated constitutional liberty. He even arranged to write a new constitution to allow his re-election.

Income redistribution and state intervention in the economy seldom work well; in Argentina, it was a disaster. Peron was finally overthrown in 1955, yet even after his removal, Argentina continued its policy of disdain for economic realities and was never able to overcome the stagnation created during Peron's reign.

In 1976, the country was taken over in a military coup, and by the late 1980s, the government was printing money to pay off its debts. This led

---

43   A 1996 movie detailed her life, with entertainer Madonna in the title role.

to rampant hyperinflation. By 1994, Argentina's "social security" (public pensions) had collapsed, and even though the payroll tax was increased to 26%, it wasn't enough—Argentina also instituted VAT (value-added tax), increased income taxes, and business taxes. It was a burden that crushed the private sector and sent the economy further into a downward spiral.

The country attempted to save seniors' pensions through privatization, but by 2001 the government had appropriated those funds as well and replaced them with defaulted government bonds. By 2002 Argentina was in an economic crisis as deep as the American Depression. The Radicals' promise of fundamental change had indeed been realized: in a single century, the country had been transformed from one of the world's richest nations to a land of poverty.

And still, the problems continued to mount—Inflation, which averaged 202% in Argentina from 1944 to 2016, rose to over 20,000% in 2016.[44]

The moral of the Argentinian story is simple: Totalitarian socialist government doesn't work. It impoverishes almost everyone except those in power. Yet modern socialists continue to condemn the next generations to poverty and misery through massive taxation and over-regulation. It has been said that Argentina throws away its future every 20 years. This is not an enviable record.

In 2016 America, supporters of socialist Bernie Sanders exhorted the people: "Get Berned." Well, Argentina, Venezuela (and others, as we'll see) have already been "Berned." The results are not pretty.

There is little doubt about the outcome of socialist policy. Unfunded, expansive government entitlements (such as Obamacare) tend to bring disaster. What remains is simply the question of how soon economic disaster catches up with good intentions. The piper must always be paid.

There was some hope for Argentina when conservative and business-friendly mayor of Buenos Aires, Mauricio Macri, was elected President of the country—the first non-Radical elected since 1916. He vowed to

---

44 http://www.tradingeconomics.com/argentina/inflation-cpi. Accessed 11/28/16.

reverse the policies of his socialist predecessors, and promised to "lift all capital controls and let the price of the currency settle in line with its market value."[45]

"Much of Latin America took a bad left detour 15 or so years ago," said the Wall Street Journal in 2015, "and it's too early to know if Mr. Macri's victory signals a larger movement back to free markets. But he can make such a shift more likely by showing that a return to the rule of law is essential to restoring broad prosperity."[46]

In 2017, *Fortune* magazine believed that Macri and his administration could "take a bow" for their first year.[47] They "unif[ied] the exchange rate, resolv[ed] the fight with international creditors, cut energy subsidies, reestablish[ed] credible statistics, and eliminat[ed] a whole host of tariffs, quotas, and export licenses."

Long term socialist policies carry long term negative effects. But if Macri had continued to set reasonable economic initiatives, the international capital markets were likely to be receptive to new debt that could help lift Argentina out of its economic quagmire.

Unfortunately, the tides turned and in the October 2019 election, and after slightly less than four years in office, Macri and his moderate running mate were soundly defeated by Alberto Fernandez, with "hyperpolarizing" ex-president Kristina Kirchner as his running mate. This happened despite the fact that Kirchner was facing trial on nearly a dozen charges of bribery, embezzlement and money laundering.[48] It looks like the Peronistas and free stuff are still appealing to voters.

45 Mary Anastasia O'Grady. "Argentina's Political Earthquake." WSJ, Opinion. 9/23/15. At A15.
46 "Reviving Argentina." WSJ, Opinion. 11/24/15. At A12.
47 http://fortune.com/2017/01/22/mauricio-macri-argentina-economy-public-spending/. Accessed 9/13/17.
48 https://www.washingtonpost.com/world/the_americas/argentinas-cristina-kirchner-facing-corruption-allegations-mounts-unlikely-comeback/2019/07/28/3f3a31d4-a3dd-11e9-a767-d7ab84aef3e9_story.html. Accessed 9/18/19.

The prognosis for Argentina is not good, but we can wish them well. New President Alberto Fernandez has said, "If I do my job right, companies will want to keep their money in Argentina."[49]

Time will tell for Argentina. We will also see if Brazil, with the election of Bolsonaro, can stem the tide of socialism—which has tended to keep much of Latin America submerged in poverty.

We must not let the creeping socialism, which debilitated Argentina happen in the U.S. Unfortunately a drift to socialism accelerated during the Obama administration. The Trump administration has reversed this trend by implementing many free-market-policies. They also tried to do so with healthcare but 51 contrarily minded Senators (all 48 Democrats and 3 Republicans), thwarted that part of the Trump agenda.

Crisis in Venezuela

Venezuela's economy was once the jewel of South America thanks to the largest oil deposits in the world. In 1973, the inflation rate in Venezuela was about 3%—similar to the U.S. average of 3.29%.[50]

By the end of 2015, it was close to 200%.[51]

What happened? Socialism.

Hugo Chavez, dictator of Venezuela from 1997-2007, was democratically elected by telling the people that socialism would make everything better. Empowered by rising oil prices, the socialist regime was able to increase spending, but at the cost of more regulations, corruption, inefficient nationalized businesses, and blind reliance on the continued flow of high-priced oil.

It was a multi-decade disaster that only picked up speed. The 2015 inflation rate has begun to look attractive compared to recent numbers:

---

49 https://www.reuters.com/article/us-argentina-mining-idUSKCN1VG1VV. Accessed 9/19/19.

50 http://www.tradingeconomics.com/united-states/inflation-cpi. Accessed 11/28/16.

51 http://www.tradingeconomics.com/venezuela/inflation-cpi. Accessed 11/28/16.

in the spring of 2018, the 3-month annualized inflation rate was 1,200,000%.[52]

While many on the left continue to promote the ideas of socialism as the way of the future, the crisis in socialist Venezuela reached the point where residents were beginning to attack grocery stores for food.[53]

Protesters are demanding greater security and free speech rights, and greater access to food and other goods—a frequent problem in socialist countries. Of course, the government blames the U.S as a destabilizing force in their country. Blaming outside influence is a tactic of radical, failed societies.

More than 2,000 graphic stories about Venezuela have been uploaded to CNN since February 2016, showing violent encounters between protesters and police. In February 2015, thousands of women marched in a protest against the government of President Maduro. The Harvard-educated opposition leader, Leopoldo Lopez, was sentenced to 14 years in prison.[54] He was released to house arrest due to health concerns in 2017.

At one point, President Obama jumped into the fray, telling the Venezuelan government that instead of making false claims against U.S. diplomats, they should focus on responding to the grievances of their citizens.

This was a "motherhood" suggestion—a feel-good platitude that misses the point of what ails Venezuela.

In the book *Atlas Shrugged* by Ayn Rand, a lead character comments, "When those that produce must ask permission from those that produce nothing, you will know that your society is doomed."[55]

---

52 https://www.forbes.com/sites/garthfriesen/2018/08/07/the-path-to-hyperinflation-what-happened-to-venezuela/#2ec97cc15e47. Accessed 7/8/19.

53 John Hinnderaker. "Socialism Crumbles in Venezuela but Democrats Think It's a Great Idea." 8/6/15. http://www.powerlineblog.com/archives/2015/08/socialism-crumbles-in-venezuela-but-democrats-think-its-a-great-idea.php. Accessed 10/22/15.

54 Eve Conant. "Behind the Headlines: Venezuela's Crisis." National Geographic Magazine. 3/2/14. http://news.nationalgeographic.com/news/2014/03/140302-venezuela-chavez-oil-protests-inflation-history-geography. Accessed 10/22/15.

55 Quoted in "I Am the Guilty Man," Charles E. Moore, The American Thinker, 10/21/13.

Sadly, this has become the Venezuelan story. Instead of building an economy based on free enterprise that takes advantage of the enormous improvements in life made possible in many parts of the world by capital and technology, Venezuela languishes. After years of misery, they have discovered what Cubans have seen for nearly three generations, and what Cicero knew two millennia ago: some governmental operating systems simply do not work.

We have witnessed the collapse of the Venezuelan state. There is no food on the shelves, and the government is restricting the use of electricity, which impacts shop owners as well as households. They have not had a fair election in over a dozen years and socialist President Maduro has said he will not relinquish power.[56] We are seeing another dictatorship consolidate power and enable oppression.

In his speech before the United Nations on September 19, 2017, President Donald Trump stated the stark truth: "The problem in Venezuela is not that socialism has been poorly implemented, but that socialism has been faithfully implemented. From the Soviet Union to Cuba to Venezuela, wherever true socialism or communism has been adopted, it has delivered anguish and devastation and failure." [57]

With the second-highest homicide rate in the world, an astonishing 90 annually per 100,000 people in 2015, many Venezuelans would likely agree.[58] [59]

There was some hope that Venezuela was emerging from their failed experiment when, in December 2015, the opposition party "trounced

56 Mary Anastasia O'Grady. "Venezuela's Maduro Won't Give Up Power." WSJ, Opinion. 11/16/15. At A17.

57 https://www.washingtonexaminer.com/trump-venezuela-in-crisis-because-socialism-has-been-faithfully-implemented. Accessed 9/18/19.

58 http://rare.us/story/three-cheers-for-venezuela-which-finally-tossed-its-socialists-out-of-power/?utm_source=DavidWebb&utm_medium=Facebook&utm_campaign=Partnership. Accessed 12/12/15.

59 92 per 100,000 in 2016, according to the L.A. Times. https://www.latimes.com/opinion/op-ed/la-oe-garzon-muggah-venezuela-violent-crime-statistics-20170331-story.html. Accessed 9/19/19.

the ruling Socialists" and took over the legislature,[60] winning a supermajority.[61]

Unfortunately, the Guido majority still faces the daunting problem that Venezuelan courts are corrupt and controlled by Maduro. And in 2016, in an effort to resolve a bitter legislative battle, three lawmakers gave up their seats, stripping Maduro's adversaries of their supermajority.

President Trump's policies have favored the private sector in Venezuela, in the hope that Venezuelans could overcome at least some of Maduro's socialist totalitarianism. It is a big job. The Venezuelan opposition must fix what the IMF considers "the world's worst-performing economy."[62]

Despite this abysmal record, many Americans continue to think Venezuelan socialism is a good thing. Ami Horowitz, the video journalist, nailed the subject through interviews with people on the street in New York City. Most had positive ideas about socialism. Then he interviewed people in Venezuela who were actually living the "dream." Watch his five-minute documentary on YouTube[63]—the difference between perception and reality is dramatic.

Leftist control of Venezuela has seriously damaged the economy and is causing increasing problems for millions of Venezuelans—a particularly tragic path for a naturally rich country with huge oil deposits. It is a classic situation where the governmental elite finds they can use the nation's wealth to buy off large parts of the population with handouts and promises of a bright future—one that lasts just long enough for the ruling elite to accumulate personal wealth in Swiss bank accounts.

---

60 "Venezuelan Opposition Thrashes 'Chavismo' in Landslide Win." The Telegraph. 12/7/15. http://www.telegraph.co.uk/news/worldnews/southamerica/venezuela/12036584/Venezuela-opposition-thrashes-Chavismo-in-landslide-win.html. Accessed 12/7/15.

61 WSJ, World News 12/9/15. At A12.

62 https://qz.com/362275/why-venezuela-is-the-worlds-worst-performing-economy-in-three-charts/. Accessed 9/21/19.

63 https://www.youtube.com/watch?v=A0ON0xUMawg. Accessed 8/28/19.

Many Venezuelans would like to see Maduro replaced, but most do not favor foreign intervention toward this goal.[64] The problem is Maduro has the guns and the opposition does not.

The Rise and Fall of the Berlin Wall

"The socialists of Eastern Germany,
the self-styled German Democratic Republic,
spectacularly admitted the bankruptcy of the Marxian dreams
when they built a wall to prevent their comrades
from fleeing into the non-socialist part of Germany."

Ludwig von Mises[65]

After the second World War, a vanquished Germany had little say in politics until 1949, when two German states emerged: East and West Germany. West Germany (the Federal Republic of Germany) was a parliamentary democracy with a capitalist economic system, freedom of religion, and labor unions. East Germany (misnamed the German Democratic Republic—there was nothing democratic about it) was a much smaller totalitarian dictatorship with communist leadership put in place by Josef Stalin.[66] In effect, it was a Soviet satellite state.

With the support of the occupying powers, the people of post-World War II West Germany experienced such rapid growth in all sectors that Germany was known as the "economic miracle." Within a short period, through hard work and a free enterprise economy, West Germans were able to build and enjoy prosperity, buy the products they wanted, and travel as they wished.

---

64 https://www.pri.org/stories/2019-01-08/venezuelans-want-president-maduro-out-most-would-oppose-foreign-military. Accessed 9/18/19.

65 Mises, Ludwig Von. *Money, Method and the Market Process.* Auburn, AL: Ludwig Von Mises Institute, 2012. At 231.

66 Josef Stalin (Iosif Vissarionovich Stalin) was the ruling dictator of the Soviet Union from the late 1920s to his death (of a stroke) in 1953.

It was the opposite in East Germany. Many of the East German assets were shipped back to the Soviet Union, as Russia considered them spoils of war. In the Eastern sector, the economy plummeted and individual freedom was severely restricted. One need only reference the GDP's of the two sectors as the years went by to see the prosperity built by capitalism, and the misery created by socialism.

This dramatic difference, of course, was apparent to both German states, and some three and a half million people eventually defected to the West in search of a better life. That flow was all but cut off with the creation of the Berlin Wall.[67]

The Wall went up in 1961 in order to confine East Berliners to the communist side of Berlin. Wherever people slept on each side of the Wall the night of August 12th is where they were confined to live for the next 28 years. Husbands and wives were separated with only slim and costly hope of reunion. Families were split. East Germans who had good-paying jobs in West Germany found themselves with no work once the wall was in place. It was an ongoing disaster for the economy of East Berlin.

During the period from 1961 to 1989, it is believed around 5,000 people escaped from East Berlin to West Berlin over the wall, including 1,300 Soviet guards. An estimated 200 people died in the attempt.[68]

An Internet search did not reveal any reports of West Berliners seeking to "escape" into communist East Berlin.

My nephew, Linden P. Blue, was asked at about age 19 why he didn't have socialistic ideas like many of his contemporaries at Stanford. His answer was that when he had gone through the Brandenburg Gates into East Berlin for the first time at age 4, he had seen the difference between life under communism and freedom. (Linden's mother had been raised in what became the Eastern Sector of Germany. The family visited relatives behind the Iron Curtain in Germany several times as he grew up.)

---

67 http://www.princeton.edu/~achaney/tmve/wiki100k/docs/Berlin_Wall.html. Accessed 12/17/15.

68 http://www.independent.co.uk/life-style/history/berlin-wall-what-you-need-to-know-about-the-barrier-that-divided-east-and-west-9847347.html. Accessed 12/17/15.

After many years of repression in East Germany, the Wall finally fell in November 1989, due to the collapse of the communist government. East Germans flooded into West Germany to much celebration around the world. The "socialist paradise" had been proven a fantasy.

The East German communist experiment lasted 28 years (August 13, 1961-November 9, 1989) until East Germany reunited (officially, on October 3, 1990) with West Germany and their democratic government.

During the entire East German experience, in spite of walls, guns, and deaths, those seeking freedom continued their efforts to escape to the free enterprise prosperity of West Berlin. Every month, sometimes every week, there were stories in the newspapers and on television of those who had escaped—or those who had been shot to death in the attempt.

A memorial was erected on the West side of the wall in honor of 18-year-old Peter Fechter, an East German who had been shot by the communists as he tried to escape, and was left on the ground to bleed to death where he fell.[69] [70]

In discussing the two Germanys and the two Koreas, commentator Kevin Grier tells us, "In both cases, the government that allowed private property and free enterprise oversaw an economic 'miracle,' while the more totalitarian governments in the pairings each produced decades of stagnation and poverty."[71]

The German people had the force of freedom on their side, and President Reagan, who was willing to say, undiplomatically, "Mr. Gorbachev, tear down this wall." Reagan's words didn't just happen and almost didn't happen at all. The words were contained in a speech draft tortuously reviewed and resisted by most of Reagan's staff, including his Secretary of State, George Shultz. The draft was written by a young

---

69 http://www.the-berlin-wall.com/videos/peter-fechter-dies-trying-to-escape-542/. Accessed 10/26/15.

70 http://coldwarsites.net/country/germany/memorial-to-peter-fechter-berlin/. Accessed 10/26/15.

71 "Empirics of Economic Growth." *The Concise Encyclopedia of Economics*, edited by David R. Henderson. Indianapolis, IN: Liberty Fund, 2008. At 145.

speech writer, Peter Robinson. Robinson is now the creator of the out-standing video series "Uncommon Knowledge" at the Hoover Institution at Stanford University. Robinson tells the story in detail in his excellent book *How Ronald Reagan Changed my Life.* From the book page 103:

> "The day the President arrived in Berlin, State and the NSC submitted yet another alternate draft. 'They were still at it on the very morning of the speech,' says Tony Dolan. 'I'll never forget it.' Yet in the limousine on the way to the Berlin Wall, the President told (Ken) Duberstein he was determined to deliver the controversial line. Reagan smiled. 'The boys at State are going to kill me,' he said, 'but it's the right thing to do.'"

One of the most significant speeches ever made affecting the freedom of the German people and ultimately the demise of the Soviet Union, was given by a President who understood the power of freedom and was not afraid to challenge diplomatic protocol with candor. It only happened because of the creative intensity of a young speech writer who loved freedom and his ultimate boss more than his job.

All too frequently the tenuous life of freedom hangs in the balance between individual creativity and the stifling forces of caution and bureaucratic protocol.

The Fall of Greece

In 2015, after a drawn-out battle to overcome the disaster of their decades-long socialist policies, which resulted in five years of recession and a 20% unemployment rate, the Greek people were given an ultimatum from the European Union: Accept our terms for austerity, or exit the EU.

Greece chose to accept, giving up their sovereignty and agreeing to the demands of their creditors, in return for a $172 billion bailout from the EU. The terms were severe, but the Greeks found them preferable to "Grexit," as the potential exit of Greece from the EU has come to be known.[72]

The key terms of the deal were:

-Debt account creation: A special debt account, whereby Greece would pay off its debtors before any government services.

-Monitoring: A permanent task force from the EU Commission would monitor implementation of reforms.

-Debt write-off: Private investors would forgive 53.5% of Greece's debt, the largest debt-restructuring plan in history.

-Eurozone contribution: Eurozone banks would agree to give up any profits they would make from Greek investments and to a reduction in Greece's interest rate from 2-3% to 1.5%.

-Debt ratio reduction: To receive the promised funds, Greece would agree to cuts in pensions, minimum wage, healthcare, defense spending and public sector jobs, with a goal to reduce debt from 160% of GDP to 120.5%.[73]

Note where the cuts were made: pensions, minimum wage, healthcare, and public sector jobs—all areas of contention in America today, and staples of socialist spending policy. Don't think that what happened in the Greek debt crisis is a European phenomenon; it could happen here. This is the very reason that conservatives push for pension reform, no minimum wage, cancellation or modification of Obamacare, and reduction of the public sector.

In the Land of Mandela

After decades of racial tension and strife, and with the guidance of Nelson Mandela, South Africa had reached miraculous compromises in a bitterly divided society.[74] In 2012, however, the African National Congress

---

72 http://www.csmonitor.com/World/Europe/2012/0221/Greek-bailout-5-key-conditions-set-by-EU/A-special-debt-account. Accessed 10/20/15.

73 http://www.theguardian.com/business/2015/jul/13/greece-bailout-agreement-key-points-grexit. Accessed 10/21/15.

74 F.W. de Klerk. "The Betrayal of Mandela's Promise." WSJ, Opinion. 8/19/15. http://www.wsj.com/articles/the-betrayal-of-mandelas-promise-1440024690?mg=id-wsj. Accessed 8/23/15.

and the unions ousted Mandela's successor and sent the country on a path that sounded suspiciously like communism: "greater state intervention in the economy, the cancellation of bilateral investment treaties with European countries, and what the ANC calls a fundamental change in the ownership and control of land."[75]

The stated goal, of course, as with all socialist governments, was to "promote equality." The result, however, is something quite different. South Africa is still one of the world's most unequal societies,[76] and their education system has been "a catastrophic failure."[77] Only the top 15% of the black population has improved living standards, while half the population earns less than 10% of the total income.

As of this writing, black South Africans are in the process of amending their constitution to allow them to seize the land and homes of white South African farmers without compensation, leaving them with nothing.[78] [79]

Cicero and the Inevitable Socialist Destination

Much has changed in the two thousand years since Cicero was assassinated for his attempts to defy Caesar's dictatorship. But one thing has remained the same: time and time again, the path of socialism leads to the very opposite of its stated goal. Instead of equality, socialism inevitably leads to a shift of wealth from the larger population to the governmental elite.

During the Russian Revolution of 1917, the communist masters traveled in private train cars with gold silverware, while they preached the

---

75   Id.

76   http://www.digitaljournal.com/article/279796. Accessed 10/21/15.

77   Miriam Mannak. "Report: South Africa Most Unequal Society." http://www.globaleducation-magazine.com/south-africa-unequal-societies-world/. Accessed 10/21/15.

78   https://www.dailymail.co.uk/news/article-6476579/South-Africa-sets-date-white-farmers-land-grab-months-announcing-test-case.html. Accessed 9/18/19.

79   https://www.bbc.com/news/world-africa-49145347. Accessed 9/18/19.

glory of communism to a people consigned to increasing poverty and, in some areas, starvation.

In Cuba, the colorful 1950s cars are not there for the benefit of tourists; they are simply the only vehicles around because Cuba has stagnated. The only people who have successful businesses are those who are in favor with the dictatorship. Fidel Castro was purportedly worth $900 million, while the Cuban economy languished under communism.

In Venezuela, the late dictator Hugo Chavez lived like a king, while his people descended further and further into poverty.

It's important to note that intention matters little in any of these cases. Freedom and progress don't come to a society from good intentions. They must be worked for and fought for. Socialism, regardless of the intention, is inevitably a destructive force that erodes freedom, and with it, any chance of lasting prosperity

As U.S. President Ronald Reagan said, freedom is just one generation away from extinction. If the 2016 U.S. election hadn't resulted in a strong shift away from the leftist policies of Barack Obama, we would have accelerated our slide toward socialist economic stagnation.

In his writings, Cicero tried to warn the Roman people and politicians of the dangers of a shift toward the values of what we now call socialism. The last defender of the Roman Republic, Cicero would eventually be killed for his beliefs, and the republic would become an empire—one that would eventually crumble under the weight of costs, crime and corruption.

Even two thousand years ago, Cicero knew that dreams of freedom are best realized in a society that values productivity, free-market incentives, and individual liberty. These are not the values of socialism.

"Stalin's gulag, impoverished North Korea, collapsing Cuba... it's hard to name a dogma that has failed as spectacularly as socialism. And yet leaders around the world continue to subject millions of people to this dysfunctional, violence-prone ideology."

-- Kevin Williamson

3

HOW NOT TO HAVE A REVOLUTION

The Failure of Cuban Communism

About a year after I was imprisoned in Cuba, the United States nego-
tiated to exchange our confiscated plane for an embargoed fishing
boat that had been paid for by the Cuban government. Our plane had
been insured by Lloyds of London, and it's possible Lloyds was involved
in the trade.

At the time, I was serving in the U.S. Air Force. Even if I could have
gone to Cuba to retrieve the plane, there was no way I was going to set
foot there again as long as Castro was in power. Instead, I paid a Denver
pilot and mechanic named Bill Truax to fly to Cuba to pick up the plane.

Bill had permission to enter the country, but he had to take repair
supplies with him. Even simple parts weren't available in communist
Cuba; Bill even had to take spark plugs and oil.

The plane was stored at Havana airport, and Bill fixed it right there
under the hostile and watchful eyes of the *barbudos*. Although he wasn't
physically harassed, the Cubans made everything as difficult for him
as they could. He ended up being there for three days to do a job that
should have taken three hours.

When Bill got back to Denver, he told me it was a much scarier experience than he expected. Although he didn't exactly fear for his life,
he definitely knew he was in a totalitarian police state and there were no
guarantees of his safety.

Despite Bill's work and the passage of only a year, the plane that came back was a wreck.[80] The Cubans had obviously been flying it—there was a bullet hole in the roof, and part of the prop had been knocked off. To avoid vibration from the now-imbalanced props, they cut down part of the other two prop blades to match—somewhat. In the end, the plane that was originally worth $50,000 (I was on the hook for it, a big deal at that time[81]), was worth about $10,000 when I got it back. I refurbished it and leased it out.

In Cuba I lost my freedom instantly and totally, and nearly lost my life. During my time there, I never knew whether I would live or die. I suffered the same torment of so many lovers of freedom who find themselves held by a communist or totalitarian state. There were no appeals to laws or courts. There was no justice. Control was absolute and complete.

I remain very fond of the Cuban people. I have a continuing problem with their abysmal authoritarian government. I recognized then what I hope we will all come to see one day: that when people lose their freedom, they are separated from a path to future prosperity. Rather than participants in an operating system that allows them to choose a future, they become victims of a system that oppresses them and denies them the advantages of a free society.

My incarceration left me with contempt for totalitarian states, and with a lifelong interest in seeing the Cuban people regain their freedom. Unfortunately, that road has been long and a dead end. The recent decades in Cuba provide a stark lesson in the failure of communism.

---

80 I have no idea what happened to the banana puree machine. It's probably still in Cuba to this day.

81 $50,000 in 1962 was equivalent to over $400,000 in today's currency. http://www.dollartimes. com/inflation/inflation.php?amount=50000&year=1962. Accessed 7/31/15.

Revolution and Repression

Fulgencio Batista was ushered in as President of Cuba in 1940, and with him came the hope for a bustling democratic society. He sponsored a constitution, ruled fairly, and stepped down after his four years were up. Prosperity and calm reigned in Cuba for several years.

At the time, Cuba was on good terms with the United States, and many Americans invested there. In fact, the U.S. "was so overwhelmingly influential in Cuba that the American ambassador was the second most important man, sometimes even more important than the Cuban president."[82]

The close U.S./Cuba relationship has come naturally since at least 1780. Geographical proximity is one reason. But the U.S.A might not have prevailed in our revolutionary war had it not been for Cuban support. The British were blockading our ports depriving Washington's forces of desperately needed supplies. Francisco Saavedra de Sangronis, a key Spanish official in the Caribbean, was instrumental in the combing of Spanish and French war ships for an assault on the British blockade and arranging a 500,000 peso loan from Cubans so the French fleet could continue north to Virginia. French and Spanish naval support was crucial to Washington's success at the Battle of Yorktown.

Prior to Castro, Cuba "was one of the most advanced and successful countries in Latin America."[83] The capital, Havana, was a "glittering and dynamic city" with a high standard of living, second in Latin America only to Venezuela, even though there were pockets of poverty in the countryside.

But in 1952, Batista did a turnaround and launched a coup to re-take power by force, effectively destroying the democratic republic he had helped to create. From 1952 to 1958, unrest spread throughout the country, and Cubans from all walks of life united against Batista. The

---

82 Earl T. Smith, former U.S. Ambassador to Cuba, during his 1960 testimony to the United States Senate. Segment on Ernesto "Che" Guevara, Douglas Kellner, *World Leaders Past and Present*, Chelsea House Publishers (1989) New York, p. 66.

83 http://www.pbs.org/wgbh/amex/castro/peopleevents/e_precastro.html, accessed 9/13/14.

stage was set for revolution, and the door opened for Castro's communist coup. By the time Fidel Castro took over on January 1, 1959, Batista had fled the country with his family. Within days, Castro's forces arrived in Havana and installed a socialist state.

When Castro fought for his revolution in the Sierra Maestra mountains, he had declared, "Our political philosophy is representative democracy and social justice in a well-planned economy."[84] These soon proved to be empty words—propaganda used to sway opinion toward him.[85] As soon as he was in power, with Che Guevara as his alter ego, Castro implemented a severe totalitarian communism, which meant most property rights and economic freedom vanished.

He claimed he would never become a dictator, but would step down if the people wished.[86] [87] Instead, he ruled with an iron hand as a dictator for 57 years.

The half-century of repressive conditions that prevailed after the Castro revolution of 1959 provides an urgent and instructive lesson on the inevitable failure of communism.

One of the most credible accounts of the horrors Castro perpetrated on his people appears in *Against All Hope: A Memoir of Life in Castro's Gulag* by Armando Valladares.[88] He recounts the constant torture the barbudos carried out on their prisoners and the numerous, brutal executions he witnessed.

Another description of Castro's ruthless regime comes from Juan Reinaldo Sanchez, originally part of Castro's elite team of security specialists. When his brother hopped a raft for Florida, Sanchez was

---

84 Id.

85 These same types of flowery promises were uttered by the Socialist presidential hopeful in 2016 and 2019, Bernie Sanders.

86 Georgie Ann Geyer, "Guerrilla Prince: The Untold Story of Fidel Castro." Little Brown & Company (1991); Garrett County Press Digital Editions (2011). www.gcpress.com   According to the author, this book was compiled from over 500 oral histories collected from those with direct knowledge of the events.

87 http://www.latinamericanstudies.org/cuban-rebels/voices.htm. Accessed 11/1/14.

88 NY: Encounter Books, 2001.

imprisoned for two years and tortured. He fled to the U.S.A in 2008, the only member of Castro's personal escort ever to defect.

In his book, Sanchez says he "came to realize that Fidel used people and then disposed of them without the slightest qualms."[89]

The Ex-Patriots Regroup: The Bay of Pigs

Cuban refugees who escaped to the United States never gave up hope of taking down Castro. They bonded together and trained in Guatemala with the support of the CIA, forming a potentially formidable force of about 1200 men.

The plan, conceived during Republican President Eisenhower's presidency, was given the go-ahead by Democrat John F. Kennedy soon after he became president. The goal was to gain a beachhead at the Bay of Pigs (Playa Girón) and then encourage an internal revolt against the Castro regime. My friends Domingo Trueba, Ñongo Puig and many others who had fought with Castro in the Sierra Maestra, had switched sides to the opposition when it became obvious that Castro was implementing a communist system. Domingo was the contact inside Cuba who would coordinate an insurrection once a successful beachhead was established. Ñongo had been working with Domingo to make this happen.

Playa Girón offered swamps on both sides of the beach that would protect the rebel patriots' flanks and force Castro's defenders to concentrate. Airstrikes from the new revolutionaries would annihilate Castro's forces.

The Cuban ex-patriot forces, led by Pepe San Roman and others including my friend Carlos E. Fonts,[90] a frogman during the invasion, prepared in Guatemala and launched from Puerto Cabezas, Nicaragua. Air support, so essential to the success of the plan, was to be provided by World War II vintage B-26 medium bombers.

---

89 Mary Anastasia O'Grady. "The Secret Life of Fidel Castro." Wall Street Journal, The Americas. 7/7/15.

90 Currently Managing Director of AdvancEnergy in Dallas.

On April 17, 1961, Brigade 2506 (the pro-American military arm of the Democratic Revolutionary Front) invaded Cuba, landing at Playa Girón.

The first air raid, which had been conducted a couple of days earlier, successfully destroyed half of Castro's air force. The second raid was supposed to destroy the rest, and allow the free Cuban patriots to win the beachhead.

However, between the first and second raid, Adlai Stevenson, the U.S. Ambassador to the U.N., and others including Secretary of State Dean Rusk, urged President Kennedy to cancel the air support on the ground that disclosure of the U.S. role in the invasion could be embarrassing. It was a difficult decision for the young President. In the end, he canceled the most important tactical part of the invasion.

The CIA knew this change would doom the offensive, and they strongly protested the order to stand down—without success. A U.S. carrier battle group over the horizon was in place as a contingency, but they also were ordered by Kennedy to stand down.

Confined to the swamps without control of the air, it was like shooting fish in a barrel. The free Cuban patriots were either slaughtered by Castro's weakened but still capable air and ground forces, or they were captured and imprisoned.

If the invading pro-U.S.A. Cuban forces had had air superiority, they almost certainly would have won, and Cuba would have thrown off the communist yoke. Instead, Kennedy's cancellation of the air raid gave the Cuban people three generations, and counting, of Fidel Castro and his oppressive regime.

The Cuban people would have risen up against Castro if they had a chance, but any efforts at an insurrection would have been suicidal after the failed invasion. For their courageous attempt to resist Castro's tyranny, Domingo and many other Cuban patriots did lose their lives.

Similarly today, moderate Muslims would rise up against radical jihadists if they didn't fear for their lives and the lives of their families.

At home in the U.S., failure of the Bay of Pigs invasion was a major embarrassment for foreign policy and nearly took the world to nuclear Armageddon soon after.

The Cuban Missile Crisis

Failure of the U.S.-supported Bay of Pigs invasion was largely responsible for the Cuban missile crisis a year and a half later, in October of 1962.

Nikita Khrushchev, Soviet leader at the time, saw Kennedy as "weak and vacillating" and Khrushchev sensed an opportunity. He told a group of Soviet advisors that Kennedy didn't "have the courage to stand up to a serious challenge."[91]

Khrushchev made a deal with Castro to install intermediate-range ballistic missiles (IRBMs capable of reaching about two-thirds of the U.S. mainland), armed with nuclear warheads, 90 miles from the USA. Many more were on their way by ship.

In mid-October, photographs taken by a USAF U2 spy plane showed that Khrushchev "had broken his promise not to deploy offensive weapons in Cuba."[92]

Kennedy and Khrushchev engaged in a "war of nerves," while the U.S. Air Force pilots conducted more than 100 missions over the Cuban missile site. Tension continued to build. At one point, the Secretary of Defense, Robert McNamara, said: "I thought it was the last Saturday I would ever see."[93]

At last, convinced by "crystal clear" photographs that Khrushchev had in fact positioned armed missiles within range of the U.S., Kennedy played the only card he had to stop further missile placements: On October 22, 1962, he ordered the Navy to set up a naval blockade to stop the Russian convoy bearing more IRBMs and nuclear warheads.

---

91 John T. Correll. "High Noon." Air Force magazine, October 2012. At 34.

92 Michael Dobbs. *The Photographs That Prevented World War III.* Smithsonian magazine, October 2012, at 1.

93 http://www.history.com/topics/cold-war/cuban-missile-crisis. Accessed 7/31/15.

Doing so was considered an act of war. During a five-day confrontation broadcast around the world, Cuba shot down a U.S. reconnaissance plane, killing the pilot. Kennedy declined to retaliate.

Khrushchev Blinks

At the time, many felt that the Soviets were stronger militarily than the U.S., but it was later verified that we had a greater supply of missiles.[94] Khrushchev calculated that nuclear action against the U.S. could result in retaliation that could annihilate his own country, and at 9 a.m. on October 27, Khrushchev "blinked." He communicated through Radio Moscow that he was "dismantling the weapons you describe as 'offensive'"[95] and returning them to the U.S.S.R. As part of the October deal, the U.S. had to withdraw our secret missile silos from Turkey and Italy.

Strength matters. By setting up the blockade, Kennedy passed the test of leadership he had failed a year and a half earlier during the Bay of Pigs Invasion. Nuclear Armageddon was averted—but only by a very narrow margin.

If Castro had held launch control over the missiles, intelligence has confirmed he would have launched them. Fortunately, Khrushchev was a cooler head and had a good understanding of what could happen to the Soviet Union in a nuclear exchange.

A Cuban Connection to the JFK Assassination?

The enduring fallout of Castro's rise to power may be greater than most appreciate. A Cuban intelligence officer, Florentino Aspillaga Lombard

---

94 "High Noon." At 33.

95 http://www.cubaheritage.org/articles.asp?artID=247. Accessed 1/20/16.

(who defected to the United States in 1987),[96] tells of his assignment to "listen in" on Texas on the morning of November 22, 1963.

Was Castro aware of the assassination that was about to take place?

Castro denied ever knowing Lee Harvey Oswald in the days following the assassination of John F. Kennedy. However, in a 1964 conversation with an American communist who was secretly working with the FBI, Castro let it slip that he knew Oswald had threatened to kill the U.S. President.

Brian Latell, a CIA Cuba analyst who spent 15 hours interviewing Aspillaga Lombard, concluded that "Castro and a small number of Cuban intelligence officers were complicit in Kennedy's death but … their involvement fell short of an organized assassination plot." Instead they 'exhorted Oswald,' and 'encouraged his feral militance' [sic] and devotion to Cuba.[97]

After defecting to the U.S., Aspillaga Lombard revealed to the CIA that every agent they had engaged and placed in Cuba was, in fact, a double agent working for Castro, most of them run personally by the dictator since the beginning of his regime.

A World of Challenges

Cuba is an example of what happens when we fail to deal with problems in a timely and effective manner. History repeatedly suggests that failure to resist rabid militant forces when they are small creates a much larger, potentially disastrous threat. Oppressive reparations from World War I and the appeasement of Germany early on, for example, were important factors that led to the tragedies of World War II.

Strength and action matter. The show of weakness to Cuba may also have inspired the Soviets to throw their support behind the North

---

96 Florentino Aspillaga Lombard was the "most knowledgeable" Cuban officer ever to defect to America. *See*, "Spilled Beans, a Cuban defector bears secrets." TIME magazine. 8/24/87.

97 Mary Anastasia O'Grady. "What Castro Knew About Lee Harvey Oswald." Wall Street Journal, The Americas. 11/17/13. Accessed 11/18/13. *See also*, "Spilled Beans, a Cuban defector bars secrets." TIME magazine. 8/24/87.

Vietnamese. Three weeks before his assassination, John F. Kennedy approved support of plans to mount a coup against President Ngo Dinh Diem, whose family-run political empire had been subverted by the Vietcong. The coup resulted in Diem's assassination.

Buddhists had been protesting against Diem. They were eventually subjugated by the Vietcong as well. Unrest in South Asia intensified and thousands of refugees lost their lives trying to flee the new North Vietnamese tyranny.

Although the U.S. military action had proven largely successful, we "lost" the Vietnam War because the Congress, controlled by Democrats at the time, cut off funding to the South Vietnamese troops. Without weapons and ammunition, they were soon overrun and the tragedy for the South Vietnamese intensified.

The Vietnam war did offer a chance for South East Asia to stabilize, at least for a while. Instead of dominoes starting to fall in Singapore, Laos, Indonesia, and Malaysia, the region was able to staunch the progress of communism in Southeast Asia.

But for the U.S. in Vietnam, and for the South Vietnamese, the cost was huge. When aggression is not answered, history tells us more aggression will be forthcoming.

The current Russian President, Vladimir Putin, probably felt weakness on the part of former President Obama similar to what Khrushchev sensed in Kennedy. It may have been the belief that the U.S. would do nothing to stop him that gave Putin the courage in 2015 to overrun Crimea and invade eastern Ukraine.

Today, the world is fraught with similar challenges. There is a serious possibility that ISIS, Al Qaeda, Hezbollah, Hamas, Syria, and Iran will continue to create havoc in the Middle East and trigger a major war that will not be contained within the region. Israel, Jordan, Egypt, Saudi Arabia, UAE, and other allies in the area could be decimated.

In 2013, the regime of the tyrannical Syrian President Assad was near collapse from civil war. Syria was using its weapons brutally against an opposition that had limited arms. At that time, the U.S. could have tipped the balance against Assad quickly and inexpensively by declaring a no-fly zone in Syria and supplying limited arms that had already been authorized by the U.S. Congress.

However, because of the Obama administration's reluctance to re-engage in the Middle East, that didn't happen. Some in the U.S. Defense Department also counseled that a no-fly zone wouldn't be decisive because casualties were being inflicted by Assad's tanks and artillery.

That counsel ignored the potential for a no-fly zone and a no-military-move zone that could have been inexpensively enforced by armed RPA's (remotely piloted airplanes, popularly called drones) once Assad's air force had been neutralized. Tanks, artillery and military support vehicles are easy targets for RPAs.

Had a no-fly zone been declared in 2013, it is likely that nearly 500,000 people, since killed by Assad's forces, would be alive today. It is also likely that the ISIS movement would have been squashed in its infancy and we would not have seen the disastrous conflict in Syria and Iraq (with heavy support from Iran). These consequences, including millions of refugees, may only be the beginning. We are already seeing their influence in the West, and they have vowed future attacks on U.S. assets and interests.

In Southeast Asia, China is attempting to establish claims and hegemony over the South China Sea by building islands from atolls. The Philippines and Japanese are resisting, with little effect so far. This is a kind of "fait accompli" warfare where small, incremental advances take place and become new reality before anyone can effectively resist them. It is what goes on in "phase zero" warfare. There isn't recognized warfare, but potentially big changes are happening. The Russians have shown effectiveness with this kind of warfare in Ukraine, Georgia, and Syria. The Iranians have shown themselves adept at using client states and terrorist organizations in the Middle East for similar results.

The Chinese, Russians and Iranians will likely continue to move aggressively unless and until that becomes excessively risky or expensive for them. There has always been great danger of miscalculation when our foreign policy signals have been ambivalent. The U.S. must have weapon systems that are effective, with maximum reliance on friendly indigenous forces on the ground against these low-order military confrontations so that larger risks and adverse consequences can be avoided in the future.

In 1937, the Japanese tried to establish hegemony over Southeast Asia, an effort that included invading China. The Japanese were much stronger, but after Japanese atrocities in China, Chiang Kai Shek knew he had to fight for China's life. The carnage in the region during WWII was epochal.

The situation is now reversed. The Chinese are feeling their strength and being aggressive. A miscalculation could lead to a major war in the region.

I believe a more realistic and "activist" foreign policy is needed to deal with increasingly complex, challenging, and dangerous international issues. Thomas Jefferson thought so when confronted by the Barbary Pirates. Polk thought so when confronted by Mexico's rejection of the U.S. annexation of Texas. Polk's action led to victory in the Mexican-American War and annexation of what is now the Southwestern U.S.

Truman thought so when confronted with the need, through the Marshall Plan, to establish stability and rebuild Europe and Japan after WWII. Reagan thought so when confronted by an ambitious and adventurous Soviet Union. His inspiration encouraged Germans to tear down the Berlin Wall and hasten the dissolution of the Soviet Union.

I am not suggesting the U.S. should become the world's police force. But we cannot refuse to recognize current world problems or retire behind our oceans in a day when ballistic missiles can cross those oceans at 17,000 mph, or information can do it at the speed of light. At the speed of light, Washington, D. C. is little more than a fraction of a second away from the Middle East.

If we believe that the U.S. and our institutions have much to offer the world, we should have an activist but tempered foreign policy which reflects that. We should believe in and support the hundreds of millions of people who also believe in freedom, free enterprise and democratic pluralism. They, too, want the benefits of the 21st century, where political stability has allowed technology and innovation to make life better. This contrasts dramatically with a life limited by the ideas of the 7th century.

From Cuba to Asia, and all points in between, it is our duty to recognize and support those who believe in government by consent as it has evolved in Western Civilization . . . . rather than government by coercion.

Profile in Freedom: Gloria and Emilio Estefan

Gloria María Milagrosa Fajardo was two years old when she came to Miami with her family in 1960. Her father had taken part in the unsuccessful attempt to overthrow the Fidel Castro communist government, and spent two years in a Cuban prison. Upon his release, the family left for Miami, where they lived in one room with relatives. Gloria's father joined the army and served in Vietnam.

Gloria and her mother moved from place to place while her father finished his tour in the military. Eventually, they moved back to Miami.

Emilio Estefan's mother wouldn't leave Cuba, and Emilio and his father went to Spain when Emilio was 14. His father thought they could get visas from there to America, but they ended up being stuck in Spain for a year, nearly homeless. Emilio played the accordion in local cafes to earn food money. They finally reached Miami, and Emilio's mother joined them in Miami after her father died in Cuba.

Gloria and Emilio met at a wedding, where Emilio was playing in a band. Gloria eventually joined the band, and in 1978 she and Emilio were married. Gloria became Gloria Estefan, and the name of the band changed, too.

Today, the couple live in an 8,000 square foot compound, where they regularly entertain. The band, Miami Sound Machine, won 26 Grammy awards, toured the world, and earned millions of dollars.[98]

98   WSJ, Real Estate/House Call. "Gloria and Emilio Estefan Build a Music Empire and a Family Compound." 12/1/15. http://www.wsj.com/articles/gloria-and-emilio-estefan-build-a-music-empire-and-a-family-compound-1448988567?mod=WSJ_GoogleNews&mg=id-wsj. Accessed 12/7/15.

Cuba Today

Anyone who wants a quick picture of what Cuba is really like today should read Michael J. Totten's *The Last Communist City*.[99]

Totten wanted to see the real Havana—not view the "botched utopian fantasy," but to experience communism firsthand. The view he got was even more appalling than he had imagined.

Instead of the utopian vision promulgated by Marx and Engels, he found that the economic and political elites lived in "a rarified world high above the impoverished masses."

Totten notes that Cuba was a rich country before it was pillaged by the Castro/Marxist revolution. Wealth was not held solely by the elite; prosperity was relatively widespread. In the 1940s and 1950s, any Cuban could get a visa to the U.S. just by asking for it, and there were more Americans in Cuba than Cubans in America, all of whom were free to come and go as they pleased. Havana was a tourist paradise, replete with restaurants and nightclubs, and a delightful tropical climate.

Most of the good life stopped with the Castro revolution. For a while, Castro was able to sustain the illusion of a good life under communism. Castro slaughtered breeding cattle, for example, to generate enough food

99   Michael J. Totten, *The Last Communist City*. City Journal, Spring 2014. http://www.city-journal.org/2014/24_2_havana.html. Accessed 9/14/14.

for a hungry population. That's like "eating your seed corn," leaving you with nothing to plant for another crop. Of course, the efforts were not sustainable; the miserable poverty that is typical of Cuba today was already beginning.

On Christmas Day 1991, the Soviet flag flew over the Kremlin for the last time: The Soviet Union had collapsed,[100] and all the subsidies that had bolstered the already-failing Cuban economy ended abruptly.

Tourists are kept away from the squalor that is most of Havana, permitted only in the parts of the city maintained for tourists by the government. Totten found that a large percentage of tourists who visit Cuba are those who are sympathetic to its politics. Since they only see the better areas of the city, they are convinced of the beneficence of the communist Cuban government.

A bus ride just to the other side of the island can be prohibitively expensive. Buses are stopped in the middle of the road and boarded by Cuban police who check bags to be sure residents aren't carrying contraband items such as extra fish and meat, since everyone is "taken care of" by the government.

Not all Cuban citizens were as enamored of Castro's "care" as the government would have you believe. If a political system and government has a lot to offer, why would so many people keep trying to escape, in spite of the harshest possible consequences? Cuba is hailed by liberals as a successful revolution, yet for decades many have died at sea in their efforts to escape it.

In October 1980, Castro declared that those wishing to leave Cuba could do so. 125,000 people took him up on the offer, and the labor force in Miami grew by 7%.[101]

More than thirty years later, escape attempts have continued. In October 2014, two boatloads of Cubans were rescued from the waters

---

100   https://www.history.com/topics/cold-war/fall-of-soviet-union. Accessed 10/6/14.

101   William F. Shughard II. *The Concise Encyclopedia of Economics*. Edited by David R. Henderson. Indianapolis, IN: Liberty Fund, Inc., 2008. At 256.

near the Yucatan peninsula, trying to escape to the U.S.A.[102] One person died in the attempt. Countless others have tried escape during the intervening years, with many more deaths.

In America, there is no one on Death Row for disagreeing with the government. The same cannot be said for Cuba, where dissenters languish in prisons and some are put to death for expressing opinions considered treasonous by the regime.

Wally Nowinski, a reporter at www.Fortune.com, writes about his trip to Cuba.[103] He got a real taste of what Cuba is like away from the planned tourist route.

To begin with, he says that travel writers pretend the food is good. Nowinsky says his experience is that "Cuban cuisine is based on imported rice, black beans, government issue cheese product #1 and enough sugar to give you diabetes in a week. It tastes about as good as it sounds."

Eighty percent of Cuba's workforce is employed directly by the state, with an average monthly salary of about $20. Taxi drivers are the rich ones; they get cash tips. A full-time employee might cost a business $100/month. To buy a five-year-old Kia costs about $100,000.

Cuba's "modern" infrastructure dates from the Soviet era. Anything that can't be produced on the island has to be imported, which often means the black market. Cuban agriculture is all-organic, and it's a nightmare—a cautionary tale of what can happen to a country free of pesticides, GMO crops, and fertilizer. "If Cuba is the example," says Nowinski, "we're all going to starve."

Farmers can't afford tractors or pesticides. Farms are capped at 40 acres since the revolution, so they're not big enough to make a profit. And while life for those working in agriculture is bad, in cities it is frequently

---

102 Sergio Chapa, *Another Boatload of Cubans Rescued off Yucatan.* http://www.valleycentral.com/news/story.aspx?id=1091100#. VDMieRY0-ZQ. Accessed 10/6/14.

103 Wally Nowinski. "These Ten Photos Will Make You Rethink Your Trip to Cuba." http://finance.yahoo.com/news/10-photos-rethink-trip-cuba-150056047.html;_ylt=A86. JyEQ7sxWcm0AxQ4nnIlQ;_ylu=X3oDMTEyYjQyOWtnBGNvbG8DZ3ExBHBvcwMyBHZ0 aWQDQjExMTVfMQRzZWMDc3I-. 2/21/16 ; https://medium.com/@wallynowinski/10-thoughts-on-cuba-with-photos-a11a813cdc8#.ina98a2hb. Accessed 10/6/14.

worse. The 100-year-old buildings (which mostly haven't seen a coat of paint since 1989) are falling apart.

Remember that in the 1950s, before the Cuban Revolution, Cuban business people like Domingo Trueba and some American companies, operating under free-market capitalism, helped to create the beautiful glittering city of Havana. What we see in Havana today is what it has been reduced to through socialism.

Mark Frank, a longtime Cuban resident, writes in *Cuban Revelations* that during his time in Cuba, he observed blocks of deserted streets with no lights on at night and no cars on the road. Residents reported that they used to make "hamburgers out of grapefruit rinds and banana skins," and doctors set broken bones with no anesthesia.[104]

Photographs of the areas not open to tourists show how the real populace lived: in crumbling hovels with cracked doors and windows, paint long since faded away, and dark, decayed streets. My son Austin visited Cuba in 2013. His pictures showed the same sad decay.

Cuba advertises its free health care, but residents know they have to bring their own sheets and medicine to the hospital.

In the 1990s, when the economy of Cuba was so desperately failing, Castro had to grit his teeth and make "concessions to the enemy." "A crash plan to develop international tourism [called the 'special program']" was put into place.[105] He was careful, however, to keep the tourists and workers separate so the Cubans wouldn't be "tainted" by capitalistic indulgences and "easy money." The only restaurants were in private homes where only family members beholden to the regime were allowed to serve the foreigners.

The Spanish-based chain, Melía Hotels, arranged with the Cuban government to pay hotel workers a fair wage of $8-10/hr. The government agreed. The catch? Melía had to pay the government *directly* and then the government paid the workers. When the hotel workers were

---

104   *Id.*; Marc Frank. *Cuban Revelations,* Gainesville, FL: University Press of Florida, 2013.

105   *Cuban Revelations,* at 21. Accessed 9/14/14; Mary Anastasia O'Grady. "Who Benefits if the embargo is Lifted?" Wall Street Journal, The Americas. 12/21/14. Accessed 7/31/15.

asked how much they really made, the answer was about 67 cents an hour.[106]

Meanwhile, the restauranteurs could often gouge a little more out of tourists, thus becoming an elite class. Tips to service people in the tourist industry also improve the lifestyle of those who receive them. To help, Cuban ex-patriots send millions of dollars from America to their relatives in Cuba. Of the sums that arrive, the government immediately pockets 13%, one of the ways they supplement declining government revenues.

Castro's daughter, Alina Fernandez Revuelta, has been critical of her father's government. Helped by a network of international accomplices, she escaped to Spain in 1993 wearing a disguise and a wig. She later emigrated to America, wrote a book about her father,[107] and now has a talk show in Miami. She devotes each Wednesday's show to discussing Cuban politics.

The Wall Street Journal reported that Havana earns "almost $8 billion a year off the backs of the health workers it sends to poor countries."[108] The missionary doctors are never paid directly; the money is funneled through Castro's government, with the "lion's share" remaining in the hands of the regime. The Cuba Study Group in Washington reports that "these types of violations are not out of the ordinary for the Cuban government."[109]

Cubans are only allowed to watch state TV, and foreign journalists who actively oppose the communist doctrine are not allowed into the country.[110]

Mary Anastasia O'Grady of the Wall Street Journal comments: "Cubans are programmed from an early age to complain to anyone who

---

106   Michael J. Totten. *The Last Communist City*. City Journal, Spring 2014. http://www.city-journal.org/2014/24_2_havana.html. Accessed 9/14/14.

107   *Castro's Daughter: An Exile's Memoir of Cuba*, New York: St. Martin's Press, 1998.

108   Mary Anastasia O'Grady. "Cuba's Slave Trade in Doctors." WSJ, Opinion. 10/22/14.

109   Collin Woodard, correspondent for The Christian Science Monitor. 11/18/2008. http://www.csmonitor.com/World/2008/1118/p07s01-wogn.html. Accessed 8/18/15.

110   Id.

will listen that 'el bloqueo' [the American trade embargo of Cuba, in effect from 1961 until June 2015] is the cause of the island's dire poverty.

"They know it's a lie. But obediently repeating it is a survival skill. It raises the odds that the demented dictator won't suspect you of having counterrevolutionary thoughts, boot you from your job, kick your children out of school and haul you off to jail."[111]

The drastic situation in Cuba could have been alleviated by securing supplies from sources other than the United States, such as Mexico, or from other European or Latin American countries. The real problem was that they had little money to buy the supplies because productivity in Cuba is so very low.[112]

While Castro preached sacrifice to his people, the reality of his life was dramatically different. He lived large, with "a private island, a yacht, some 20 homes across the island, a personal chef, a full-time doctor, and a carefully selected and prepared diet."[113]

Fidel preached "the good of the State" to his people, yet he himself was worth some $900 million. Castro's estates were lavishly landscaped with fruit trees and he lived a life of privilege including relationships with many women outside his marriage. Meanwhile, his people starved.

After Castro's death, the New York Post published an article[114] detailing "Fidel Castro's life of luxury and ladies." It also revealed his policies of murder and humiliation of those who went against him. Even his own brother was threatened. When Raul became an alcoholic, Castro told him to shape up "and nothing will happen to you." Knowing his brother's nature, Raul sobered up.

---

111 "Who Benefits if the Embargo is Lifted?" Wall Street Journal, The Americas. 12/21/14.

112 Id.

113 Mary Anastasia O'Grady. "The Secret Life of Fidel Castro." Wall Street Journal, The Americas. 7/7/15.

114 Laura Italiano. "Inside Fidel Castro's life of luxury and ladies while country starved." The New York Post. 11/26/16. http://nypost.com/inside-fidel-castros-life-of-luxury-and-ladies-while-country-starved. Accessed 11/28/16.

The Trump administration has been much more realistic in dealing with Cuba than the previous administration. When will the communist regime that has shackled Cuba for over 60 years be overthrown?

Cuba—U.S. Relations

Just as Cuba was reeling from declining Venezuelan support, the U.S. stepped in to strengthen the Castro regime. To my great chagrin, the U.S. President, Barack Obama, referred to Castro as an inspired leader and beloved revolutionary and established normal diplomatic and trade relations with Cuba. In July 2015, a Cuban Embassy opened in Washington D.C.[115] to much fanfare.

At the time, journalist O'Grady felt the Obama administration "doesn't understand the lesson of the Cuban revolution."[116]

She's correct. The agreement between the U.S. and Cuba has done almost nothing to ease the suffering of the Cuban people. The new money that flows into the country has gone into the pockets of the communist elite; very little has trickled down to the populace. The only businesses that have opened have been for those sympathetic to the regime.

The Obama administration initiatives took the pressure off conditions that could have brought about real change for the Cuban people. We gave them privileges and lifted travel bans while ignoring the suffering Castro has caused the Cuban people for decades.

To my great relief, in 2017 President Donald Trump signed a Presidential Directive rolling back key points of the Obama-era open door policy, curtailing travel to, and commerce with, the island in the future. The regulations do not affect airlines and cruise ships, but greatly

---

115 http://www.wusa9.com/picture-gallery/news/local/dc/2015/07/20/cuban-embassy-opens-in-washington-dc/30426633/. Accessed 7/31/15.

116 Mary Anastasia O'Grady. "The Secret Life of Fidel Castro." Wall Street Journal, The Americas. 7/7/15.

diminish the possibility of investment in the country. Purchases of Cuban cigars and rum, at least for the present, are not affected.[117]

To those who would travel to Cuba, I ask that they look at 60 years of Castro totalitarianism and urge them not to do anything to support the current system. It has been a disaster for the Cuban people, and many others. It almost took us to nuclear Armageddon.

Remember that tyrannical governments need financial support to perpetuate themselves; traveling to Cuba provides that support, and allows the continuation of the Castro legacy.

"All that's going to change here is that there's going to be more money going into Cuba, meaning more money going into the pockets of these folks," Senator and former presidential hopeful Marco Rubio said. [118]

Before Castro, Cuba was the second-wealthiest country per capita in Latin America—behind only oil-rich (at the time) Venezuela. The vibrant people of Cuba and Venezuela should still be enjoying prosperity instead of numbing, frustrating and miserable poverty.

While much of the world has benefitted during recent decades through modern technology and increasing prosperity, the Cubans have had 60 years of dismal poverty caused by a socialistic/communistic economy.

Cuban cigars have tended to be in demand, but that is hardly a major boon to civilization. Cigars don't represent new business or industry. They are already relatively easy to obtain in the U.S., as Cuba exports them to other countries, which then export them here.[119] Check out any cigar bar in a major city and you'll find them there.

Cuba remains an important part of the Iran/Venezuela/Cuba axis that is destabilizing governments in this hemisphere and discouraging the ideas of pluralism, free enterprise, and government by consent that are the hope for the future. Indeed, if Cuba's intelligence and secret

---

117   https://www.cigaraficionado.com/article/president-trump-cuts-cuba-travel-changes-obama-era-rules-19441. Accessed 9/20/19.

118   Lucy McCalmont and Daniella Diaz. "Rubio Fires Back at Paul." Politico Magazine. 1http://www.politico.com/story/2014/12/marco-rubio-rand-paul-cuba-113699. Accessed 10/28/15.

119   John Tamny. *Popular Economics*. Washington, D.C.: Regnery Publishing, 2015. At 156.

police infrastructure was not there to support the Maduro government in Venezuela, it would likely collapse.

The Obama policy toward Cuba was a tragic turn of events. Sanctions were working in Cuba, and we were likely about to see a major drop in the strength of the Castro regime.

With the new ill-advised "normalization" of relations with Cuba in 2015, the Castro regime was strengthened and there was little if any increase in freedom and well-being of the Cuban people.

John Tamny comments in *Popular Economics* that "an end of the U.S. embargo would not change much. People trade products for products, and the rulers of that ailing island, by severely limiting property rights, give their people little incentive to produce."[120]

Even though the dictator is now dead, Raul Castro and his sycophants have not brought about reformist change.

The Cuba—U.S. Risk

In September 2014, an internal FBI report indicated that Cuban Intelligence is actively recruiting leftist professors and agents in the U.S. as spies and influence peddlers.[121] Cuban Intelligence actively pursues academics in America, who are known for their leftist leanings. "Cuba heavily targets the schools that train the best candidates for U.S. government jobs, like Georgetown University, Johns Hopkins University, and George Washington University," says Chris Simmons, a retired spy catcher for the Defense Intelligence Agency.

Cuba's hope is that some of these academics may enter government service and be of use to Cuba as spies or leftist members of the U.S. Deep State.

---

120   Id.

121   Bill Gertz, FBI: Cuban Intelligence Aggressively Recruiting Leftist American Academics as Spies, Influence Agents; http://freebeacon.com/national-security/fbi-cuban-intelligence-aggressively-recruiting-leftist-american-academics-as-spies-influence-agents. Accessed 9/15/14.

U.S. Government officials who deny or ignore this activity risk endangering U.S. national security. The Trump administration has not been blind to the dangers.

Cuba's Uncertain Future

The iron grasp of Fidel Castro and his communist regime has strangled Cuban prosperity for more than half a century. To maintain control, Castro refused to allow internet access or news from the outside to "taint" his communist utopia. Cubans knew little of the progress taking place all over the world, particularly in free societies.

In 2008, Castro's brother Raul was elected president and took over from the ailing Fidel, but things didn't change much.

In November 2016, Fidel Castro died at age 90. In the streets of Miami, Florida, thousands of ex-patriot Cubans came out to celebrate the demise of the hated dictator. Most of them had personal horror stories to relate, of this brutal tyrant who murdered thousands and kept his communist island republic in a state of poverty and ignorance

Because of the new policy of rapprochement, Cuba is currently allowing people to leave without restraint. Mirroring the 125,000 who gained freedom in 1980, thousands are now arriving on Mexico's border, and coming through Costa Rica. "There are thousands more on the way behind us," said one 38-year old father who crossed from Guatemala on his way here. "Everyone wants to go now while it is possible," he said.[122] The number of Cubans escaping to the U.S. in 2015 was over 43,000.[123]

Apparently, those escaping don't hold much hope that the renewed diplomatic relations with America will do much to help the Cubans.

---

122 Dudley Althaus. "Cubans Flood Mexico in Bid to Reach U.S." WSJ, World News. 11/17/16. At A14.

123 Nick Miroff. The Washington Post. 12/5/15. https://www.washingtonpost.com/world/the_americas/the-other-migrant-crisis-cubans-are-streaming-north-in-large-numbers/2015/12/05/3160772e-992f-11e5-aca6-1ae3be6f06d2_story.html.

The 1966 Cuban Adjustment Act[124] allows those escaping Cuba to apply for asylum and generally receive a green card within a year. As of 2017, approximately 2.3+ million Cubans reside in our country. [125] I am happy for those who experience the freedom of the U.S., but I pray for the day when all Cubans breathe the air of freedom.

The real answer for the future is to give Cuba back to free people so that they can resurrect a free market economy.

As is typical of any socialist/communist society, the only ones who thrive—and survive -- are the government elites.

Another famous individual phrased it this way:

"We shall banish want, we shall banish fear.
The essence of National Socialism is human welfare rooted in a fuller life for every German from childhood to old age."

- Adolph Hitler

The difference between Nazi National Socialism and Marxist Socialism? Not much.[126]

I can never forget my experience in communist Cuba and the loss of valiant and strong Cubans like Domingo and Ñongo. I look forward to the day when Cuba will join the world with a free economy and democratic political institutions.

---

124 http://immigration.about.com/od/usimmigrationhistory/fl/What-Is-the-Cuban-Adjustment-Act-of-1966.htm.

125 https://factfinder.census.gov/faces/tableservices/jsf/pages/productview.xhtml?pid=ACS_17_1YR_B03001&prodType=table. Accessed 9/20/19.

126 For a fascinating discussion of the similarities between Nazism and socialism, see "Why Naziism was Socialism and Why Socialism is Totalitarian" at the Mises Institute site. https://www.mises.org/library/why-nazism-was-socialism-and-why-socialism-totalitarian. Accessed 9/15/17.

Profile in Freedom: Marco Rubio

Reading the signs of what was to come, Senator Marco Rubio's parents fled Cuba in 1956 and took menial labor jobs in the U.S. to support themselves. Marco's father worked as a bartender, his mother as an industry service worker. Their futures were made possible through the economic freedoms of the U.S., where they nurtured three children.

The Rubios longed for many years to return to the Cuba they knew, the Cuba of their childhood. For a time, Marco's mother did return there with Marco's older siblings to see if they could reestablish their lives. But it was not to be. Castro had declared Cuba a Marxist state, and the living conditions were squalid. Mrs. Rubio and Marco's older siblings returned to the U.S. in 1961, and Marco was born in 1971.

After obtaining a law degree from the University of Miami in 1993, Marco was elected in 1998 to the West Miami City Commission. In 1999 he won a seat in the Florida House of Representatives, and became Speaker of the House at 28. In 2011, he was elected to the United States Senate as junior Senator from Florida.

Rubio's philosophical beliefs and ideas on civil government were first planted by a family who had lost their native country. They understood the importance of U.S. ideas about freedom, free enterprise, and hard work in building productive lives for themselves and their children.

In 2015, the boy who grew up in a poor, ex-patriot Cuban family became a candidate for President of the United States.

4

SWEDEN'S DECLINING FOUNDATION

The Myth Of Swedish Socialism

Advocates of socialism who defend its undeniably tragic track record often make two related claims. The first is that socialism really *has* worked, and that the evidence can be found in a specific, flourishing country. The second claim is that we can simply copy that operating system to other nations, so they can likewise flourish.

In this chapter we'll examine the case of Sweden, long-lauded as a socialist success story, to see how that claim stands up to scrutiny.

When Capitalism was King

The missing piece from most stories of Swedish socialism is the fact that it is a relatively recent phenomenon.

From about 1870 to 1950, Sweden was one of the *least* economically regulated countries in Europe, and enjoyed small government.[127] There were low taxes and a pro-business environment, and the country still benefitted from a great work ethic and egalitarian spirit, *laissez-faire* economic policies, and the exponential gains of the First Industrial Revolution.

---

127 Janos Kornai, Reforming the State: Fiscal and Welfare Reform in Post-Socialist Countries. Cambridge University Press, 2001. At 145-6.

The Sweden of the day was a "decentralized, capitalist market system, highly open to international trade," and boasted high mobility of capital and labor.[128] Until 1950, the country had one of the highest per capita incomes in the world,[129] and in the years after World War II, Swedish unemployment hovered at only 4%. For decades, Sweden was one of the freest countries in the world, and government spending relative to GDP was around 10%,

Change, however, was looming. Welfare-state provisions began in the 1950s and 60s, and by about 1970 the total public sector spending had increased to 40 percent.[130] From 1970 to 1985, large and centralized government arrived, along with socialist-style regulations. In 1975, the Swedish Parliament made the decision to change Sweden from a homogenous culture of primarily those born and raised in Sweden with similar upbringing, values, and traditions, into a "multi-cultural" state.

Under the influence of socialist politicians, government spending eventually increased further to an unsustainable 65-70% of GDP.

The Capitalist Trust Fund

At this point, socialist pundits generally point to Sweden's high global per capita GDP and happiness levels, and declare victory. The problem is that the socialist reforms in Sweden are relatively recent, and their effect has yet to be seen because of the enduring benefit of previous decades of free-market capitalism.

Writing for the Mises organization, Per Bylund observes that, "... Sweden's welfare state 'worked' through the early 1970s thanks to deliberately preserving capitalist institutions and expanding its scope at a slower rate than the country's overall economic growth."

128   *Id.*, at 146.

129   http://www.csmonitor.com/Business/Stefan-Karlsson/2012/0912/Are-free-markets-the-secret-to-Sweden-s-success. Accessed 9/19/14.

130   Janos Kornai, Reforming the State: Fiscal and Welfare Reform in Post-Socialist Countries. Cambridge University Press, 2001. At 147.

In other words, because Sweden continued its minimal regulation of businesses, those businesses prospered and provided the funding for a generous welfare state. A long, early buildup of capital made Sweden a wealthy nation. Without that capital foundation, the generous welfare reforms later awarded could not have been funded — socialized economies simply aren't very productive. There's that "other people's money" concept again. Government does not produce wealth—it operates from the taxes of people who do. Without the tax base, a socialist economy eventually flounders.

If such a system *could* have worked, Sweden would have been the place, for several reasons:

- A small country is easier to manage. Sweden's population was around 10 million in 2017, contrasted with about 326 million in the U.S. The state of California has more than four times the population of Sweden – even the County of Los Angeles alone has only slightly less than the entire country of Sweden.[131]

- The lack of inheritance taxes in Sweden, [132] as well as other capitalist provisions, encourages investment and savings. That is good for business formation, job creation, and high wages.

- Sweden also has no minimum wage law or wealth tax.[133] These are circumstances generally found in a free-market economy, where business growth and wealth accumulation are encouraged.

There is a singular characteristic that further defines the unique nature of the Swedish nation: During the period from 1870 to approximately 1970, public sector administrators seem to have been relatively

131   http://worldpopulationreview.com/us-counties/ca/los-angeles-county-population/.

132   http://taxfoundation.org/article/estate-and-inheritance-taxes-around-world. Accessed 11/27/15.

133   http://www.forbes.com/sites/timworstall/2011/08/20/ paul-krugman-and-the-socialist-hellhole-that-is-sweden/.

honest. Some attribute this to high wages; at the turn of the 20th century, public administrators earned 12–15 times the average industrial worker's salary.[134] This honesty "evolved into a social norm"[135] which was incorporated into the Lutheran work ethic.[136] (In 2015, Sweden was still 87% Lutheran. The percentage dropped to 58% in 2019, and will no doubt continue to decline.)[137] [138]

All of this points to one conclusion: Sweden is, in essence, still surfing a wave of free-market prosperity that crested decades ago, while continuing to benefit from a trust fund of cultural attitudes and wealth built by previous generations.

As with all trusts that are abused, however, the Swedish legacy is being slowly eroded. There is now double taxation in some cases in Sweden, and massive regulation. This makes it difficult for small firms to flourish and new ones to be created.

There are approximately 600 companies in Sweden. In Connecticut, which has a population more or less equal to Sweden, more than 300,000 businesses are currently active,[139] 19 of which are Fortunate 500 companies.[140] If Swedish companies begin to produce substantial profit and bear the burden of the massive Swedish tax system, one wonders whether they might seek greener pastures in more business-friendly countries. Further, "While America's economic problems cannot be ignored, it is noteworthy that Scandinavia's progressive tax systems fail to protect their citizens from staggering personal debt."[141]

---

134 Janos Kornai, Reforming the State: Fiscal and Welfare Reform in Post-Socialist Countries. Cambridge University Press, 2001. At 148.

135 Id.

136 http://www.mrconservative.com/2013/03/5847-swedish-socialism-falls-apart; http://eura-relocation.com/?p=cultural.guide.to.the.swedes.

137 The CIA World Factbook 2015. NY: Skyhorse Publishing, 2014. At 705.

138 https://sweden.se/society/10-fundamentals-of-religion-in-sweden.

139 http://www.gaebler.com/Number-of-Small-Businesss-in-Connecticut.htm. Accessed 9/19/19.

140 https://www.courant.com/business/hc-fortune-500-connecticut-20160606-story.html. Accessed 9/19/19.

141 https://thefederalist.com/2015/08/11/scandinavia-isnt-a-socialist-paradise. Accessed 9/18/19.

Despite Sweden's claims of Utopia, America and Sweden had virtually the same poverty rate in 2014, approximately 14%.[142] [143] By 2017, Sweden's poverty level increased to 16%.[144] The 2017 rate in America was 12.3%.[145]

Does the "Nordic Model" Transfer?

Even if we were to take the "success" of Swedish socialist policies at face value (which we clearly should not), there is little evidence to suggest that the scenario can be duplicated in other countries.

In addition to the North Sea oil wealth that has helped to sustain the "Nordic Model," Denmark, Finland, Norway and Sweden are distinguishable by "a unique culture built upon trust, a Lutheran work ethic and strong emphasis on personal responsibility….and healthy lifestyles."[146] That culture has given the Nordic countries relative freedom from the corruption that plagues socialist operating systems. Unfortunately, transplanting that system elsewhere is unlikely to succeed.

"The bad news for the rest of the world," comments economist Kevin D. Williamson, "but especially for highly complex societies such as the United States, India and China – is that the social conditions that produce these high levels of trust are not generally transmutable."[147]

There is no shortage of evidence to support Williamson's point. In 2009, a Gallup poll showed that 81% of Americans only trust the

142   https://theodora.com/wfbcurrent/sweden/sweden_economy.html. Accessed 9/19/19.

143   https://www.census.gov/library/publications/2018/demo/p60-263.html. Accessed 9/19/19.

144   https://www.eapn.eu/wp-content/uploads/2019/01/EAPN-EAPN-SE-Poverty-Watch-2018-En-Final.pdf. Accessed 9/19/19.

145   https://www.census.gov/library/publications/2018/demo/p60-263.html. Accessed 9/19/19.

146   Nima Sanandaji. "The End of Nordic Illusions." WSJ, Opinion/Commentary. 6/24/15. http://www.wsj.com/articles/the-end-of-nordic-illusions-1435166752?alg=y&mg=id-wsj. Accessed 10/20/15.

147   Kevin D. Williamson, *The Politically Incorrect Guide to Socialism*. Wash. D.C.: Perseus/Regnery, 2011. At 102.

government "some of the time."[148] With statistics like that, the Swedish model simply would not work.

A vivid example is the corruption scandal of the city of Bell, California, a blue-collar city with a large percentage of Hispanic residents, many of whose native language is not English. The median salary there is just over $35,000,[149] as contrasted against the median salary in the USA of $61,362 in 2017.[150] Two Bell officials were found guilty of misappropriating approximately 6.7 million dollars. Had the City Manager maintained his position until retirement, he would have retired with a yearly pension of $976,771, an unconscionable sum under the circumstances.

It was President Truman who said you don't get rich in politics unless you're a crook.

Another scandal involved CalPERS, the largest government worker pension fund in the nation with $296.3 billion in assets. In July 2014, their CEO pled guilty to conspiracy in an influence-peddling scandal that rocked the California capital of Sacramento.[151]

Swedish Socialism in Decline

This is where we find the "gem" of socialist idealism as of this writing: a former free-market economy with a huge trust fund and a small, unusually hardworking and ethical population, which has been the site of a socialist experiment—one that's unlikely to transfer to other countries.

And just how is the experiment faring?

Sweden is renowned for its health care system, available to all. But despite a high tax rate of about 57%,[152] it is now floundering. Like most nations who adopt socialist health care, they are now running into the same problems: long waitlists, rising costs, and rationing of services. And

---

148 http://www.gallup.com/poll/5392/trust-government.aspx.

149 https://www.payscale.com/research/US/Location=Bell-CA/Salary.

150 https://wallethacks.com/average-median-income-in-america/.

151 http://www.latimes.com/business/la-fi-calpers-scandal-20140701-story.html.

152 https://tradingeconomics.com/sweden/personal-income-tax-rate. The tax rate reached 62% in 1998.

it will only get worse, especially with the huge influx of refugees who arrive expecting state support.

One interesting statistic is that the poverty rate in Sweden is more or less the same as it is for Swedes who emigrated to America: 6.7% in 2011. Tellingly, the lifespan of a Swede in America is 2.6 years more than the average American, but the lifespan of a Swede living in Sweden is almost the same – 2.7 years more than the average American. In cases of both poverty rates and lifespan, socialism seems to have had little impact despite huge expenses and high taxes paid by citizens. [153]

Recent reforms have allowed Swedes to take advantage of private health insurance so they are not restricted solely to the reduced and rationed public health care. In America, with Obamacare, we don't seem to have learned the lesson – it took us in the opposite direction. Once an entitlement such as Obamacare becomes established, politically, it becomes almost impossible to get rid of it – despite its debilitating effects on the cost and quality of health care. President Trump is doing his best to reverse the effects but is blocked at almost every step by the Democrats and a few Republicans.

Like healthcare, education is universally available in Sweden. And, like other government sponsored programs, it is failing to deliver.

In a perhaps surprising statistic, "Sweden's public education system is ranked lower than that of the United States. According to the OECD, Sweden ranks 30 of 37 in math and 24 of 37 in reading. The United States, meanwhile, is 27 of 37 in math and 25 of 37 in reading. Norway and Denmark are both ranked better than the United States, but not by much. These realities destroy the pervasive myth that "socialist" Scandinavian schools are the best in the world.

Despite what [2016 & 2020 socialist democratic candidate] Bernie Sanders might believe, educational institutions in Sweden are not superior to those in the United States. Sweden's high tax rates have not ensured

153   Victoria Buhler, Sweden is No Socialist Paradise. Adam Smith Institute, Blogs. 6/23/11. http://www.adamsmith.org/blog/international/sweden-is-no-socialist-paradise. Accessed 9/10/15.

educational excellence, and many Swedes likely pay the equivalent of college tuition for their children in the form of taxes.

Even though students pay no tuition, each student still ends up with around $19,000/year in debt for other personal expenses they have to shoulder.

Alex Newman, an American journalist who has lived all over the world and currently resides in Sweden, had this to say on his blog: "This socialist system seeks to destroy the middle class, to control the education of our children, to destroy the independent thinker and to crush the human spirit, all under the guise of equality for all."[154]

The tragic 2011 case of Domenic Johansson demonstrates Sweden's current obsession with ensuring that children are indoctrinated into "statist" principles.[155] Seven-year old Dominic Johansson was yanked off a plane by Swedish social workers as his parents were attempting to move from Sweden to India because Sweden would not allow the Johanssons to home-school their child. [156]

Almost seven years later, the Swedish government still maintains custody of Domenic to keep its hold on the mind of its young national. Recently, a court ruled that parental rights would not be terminated, affirming that Domenic gets proper care from his parents, and in response to vociferous public outcry.[157]

The parents are hopeful they will be reunited with their son one day. Meanwhile, their little boy remains in Swedish foster care for no reason other than his parents wanted the right to decide his schooling. His foster parents have told him he will never be reunited with his family.

In recent years, the Swedes have drifted toward suppression of religious freedom, educational liberty, and the traditional family, with the

---

154 http://www.redicecreations.com/radio/2012/06/RIR-120617.php#.T9-njQMJ0uc.blogger. Accessed 10/20/15.

155 "Parents of Boy Seized by State Hopeful After Favorable Court Ruling." 6/14/12. http://www. hslda.org/hs/international/Sweden/201206140.asp. Accessed 9/10/15.

156 http://freesweden.net/sweden_unmasked.html. Accessed 9/18/19.

157 https://sites.google.com/site/homeschoolinginsweden/sweden---the-next-germany-/the-state-abduction-of-dominic-johannsson. Accessed 10/20/15.

ideas of the State replacing those of religion. This is not atypical of socialist societies; when the government controls economic life, that control tends to spread to other areas as well. In Sweden, the State daycare system now cares for more than 90% of the children older than 18 months.[158]

When supporters present Sweden as such a wonderful country with so many well-run state services, I wonder if they are fully aware of the lack of intellectual, educational and religious freedom. Attorney Mike Donnelly, Director of International Affairs for the U.S.-based Home Schooling Legal Defense Fund, states that Sweden is near the bottom of the world list in terms of educational freedom, in the company of North Korea and communist China.[159]

The cracks in the Swedish system are beginning to show in other areas, too. The previously solid work ethic, so notably present in Sweden, is beginning to waver. According to polls "about half of all Swedes now think it is acceptable to call in sick for reasons other than sickness."[160] Just a generation ago, this would have been unthinkable.

There is also a high rate of alcoholism in Sweden and a tragic rate of 13 suicides per year per 100,000 people. Nordic countries, in general, have the highest suicide rates.[161]

When Economist Friedrich Hayek was interviewed in the 1970s, he said of Sweden: "There is perhaps more social discontent in Sweden than in almost any other country I have been. The standard feeling that life is really not worth living is very strong in Sweden."[162]

158 Jonas Himmelstrand. "How Sweden's Mass State-Funded Daycare System is Actually Hurting Kids." 9/16/15.

159 Id. http://www.crisismagazine.com/2011/swedens-big-government-utopia-unmasked

160 Kevin D. Williamson. *The Politically Incorrect Guide to Socialism*. Wash. D.C.: Perseus/Regnery, 2011. At 108.

161 Maia Szalavitz. TIME magazine. 4/25/11. http://healthland.time.com/2011/04/25/why-the-happiest-states-have-the-highest-suicide-rates/. Accessed 12/12/15.

162 Wapshott, at 289, quoting from 1977 interview with Thomas W. Hazlett.

Failing to Compete

The failure of socialism isn't just internal. While state-funded platforms like the Swedish health care and education systems often deliver sub-par results, there is a broader context for the impact of excessive state control.

Socialist operating systems—even that of Sweden's, which is not completely socialist—tend to be shackled by high taxes and excessive bureaucracy. That, in turn, makes socialist countries less competitive in world markets.

Changes in technology have meant increasing globalization across many fields. The USA has managed to maintain its competitiveness largely by being technically creative. Much of Europe has lost that edge, however, and some suffer economically because social welfare and socialistic systems have eroded their incentives for profit.

The economy of neighboring Norway is more or less propped up by North Sea Oil revenues, and Sweden has been heavily involved in the North Sea exploration. North sea oil fields are being depleted. In writing about Scotland's (failed) vote on independence from Britain, one commentator wondered whether dependence on North Sea Oil for extended funding is well placed, since, "the North Sea reserves are long past their peak and could be headed for a steep decline."[163]

Will Sweden ever be broadly competitive again? Would Sweden be the first choice for new factories or other capital ventures? Probably not, if international competitiveness is the criterion.

One young blogger bemoans the drunken evenings (every evening, he claims), when Swedes get drunk at home before going out because alcohol is too expensive to buy in bars or restaurants. Alcohol is sold in government shops and is highly taxed.

Workers in Sweden clock an average of 1,400 hours a year (versus an average of 1,800, nearly 30% more, in the U.S.), and when out of work

---

163   Griffe Witt, *The Washington Post*, 9/14/14; http://bastiat.mises.org/2014/01/turing-their-backs-on-swedens-welfare-state, accessed 8/26/14.
http://www.washingtonpost.com/world/europe/scotland-bets-on-north-sea-oil-even-as-the-wells-start-to-run-dry/2014/09/13/e61edfd9-d0ec-4bb2-826b-38c76bb113aa_story.html; accessed 9/16/14.

they receive high unemployment checks, which provide a disincentive to look for work. As of June 2019, the unemployment rate in Sweden is 7.6%.[164]

Housing rates continue to soar, much to the chagrin of regulators.[165] The average household debt is 172% of income after taxes. "The tax code is in the hands of politicians, as are the planning and rent-control regimes that impede the construction of new homes. An independent commission last year recommended urgent reforms to all three, but has been ignored."[166]

William L. Anderson, of the Mises Organization,[167] summarizes as follows:

> "The European welfare states are *not* making their citizens wealthier. Over time, the cracks in these relatively wealthy nations are growing larger, and if the disease is not arrested, much of Europe will tumble off into real poverty in the not-so-distant future. Europeans -- and, most likely, Americans -- seem destined to learn the hard way that large, seemingly intractable welfare systems have their way of destroying the Goose that Laid the Golden Eggs."[168]

As with most historic examples, countries like Sweden are seeing the unfortunate economic results of welfare state policies. Income inequality is also on the rise. But there is nothing incompatible, says Kevin

---

164 https://tradingeconomics.com/sweden/unemployment-rate.

165 "Home is Where the Heartache Is." The Economist. 11/7/15. http://www.economist.com/news/finance-and-economics/21677671-house-prices-sweden-continue-soar-regulators-despair-home-where. Accessed 11/27/15.

166 *Id.*

167 www.mises.org

168 William L. Anderson. Mises Institute. 5/9/02. "Sweden: Poorer Than You Think." https://mises.org/library/sweden-poorer-you-think. Accessed 12/1/15.

Williamson, with having a higher standard of living in a country where income inequality is rising. As John Hawkins notes:

> "Having real freedom means you get to make real choices and when that happens, some of those choices will work out better than others. The only way to change that is to build a massive government apparatus that makes everyone poorer in return for reducing the amount of natural inequality that will happen when people are allowed to pursue their wildly differing hopes and dreams."

Capitalism is not perfect, but it won't bankrupt the country, it doesn't reward failure and it can't control you like socialism.

Beginning in 2006, Sweden seemed to be moving toward more capitalistic economic policies. There were relatively extensive tax cuts, a partial turn away from the socialist welfare system. The retirement age was raised to 70 to ease some of the burden from the system.[169]

Some other reforms include:

- Reducing the corporate business tax rate;

- Cutting the minimum capital requirement for limited liability companies in half;

- Making it easier to register property;

- Reducing taxes on payroll and profit;

- Making it easier to get credit;

- Putting time limits on resolving commercial disputes.

---

169 John Micklethwait and Adrien Wooldridge, "In Search of Gladstonian Republicans," WSJ, Opinion, 5/30/14, accessed 9/16/14.

All of these free enterprise basics tend to create a stronger business environment, and an enterprise resurgence seems to be underway. A number of "unicorns" (startups worth more than $1 billion) have recently been created in Sweden.[170]

Game companies are booming in Sweden, likely due to capitalistic improvements in business regulation. In addition, government of the 1990s subsidized computers for every family in the country and children grew up with them. Long, dark winters make gaming more attractive.[171]

While the average net salary in Sweden is around US$40,000, [172] there are a number of billionaires in Sweden. Much of the funds for these enterprises came from a time when Sweden was a rich capitalist country. Remember that the major players in Sweden—Volvo, IKEA, and Alfa Laval—were all created during the earlier pro-business environment.

So what do we deduce from this? It is simple, says Victoria Buehler of the Adam Smith Organization: "[G]rowth and wealth creation [are] best left to individual entrepreneurs, and the best action the government can take is to create a pro-business environment in which these individuals have the highest chance of success."

Success in Sweden cannot be attributed to a socialist government. Capitalistic Sweden built considerable wealth before 1950 based on its moral foundation, and a free profit-oriented work ethic. Swedes enjoy property rights enforcement, free trade, and investment and financial freedoms similar to the United States—freedoms, in other words, that are similar to capitalist societies, not socialist ones. The Swedish model is really a cooperative agreement between government, unions, and private industry. It works somewhat in Scandinavia, but there are few favorable examples elsewhere.

Sweden does not have pure Marxian socialism, but they have a welfare state that Swedes in the private sector are willing to live with. Even

---

170   http://www.huffingtonpost.com/helen-i-hwang/how-stockholm-became-a-un_b_8581896. html. Accessed 11/21/15.

171   http://swedishstartupspace.com/2013/09/23/sweden-game-development/. Accessed 11/28/15.

172   https://www.averagesalarysurvey.com/sweden. Accessed 11/28/15.

so, the question remains: Is it the best model for the future? The system is showing signs of stress, and there have been deep cuts in public spending. This had become reality even under the former, more liberal government.

Socialism is a zero-sum game. You can't have socialism without taking from the productive to support the unproductive, and the result is a downward spiral where a failure to compete slowly drains what resources a country does have.

Now, Sweden faces a new challenge. Not only is a competitive world challenging their ability to be productive, but the same world is challenging the once-homogenous nature of the country itself. Many of the former arguments in favor of Sweden may no longer be valid due to their immigration policies .

A Changing Sweden

Sweden is well known for its high immigration, and once welcomed more refugees per capita than any other EU nation.[173] Since the 1980's, a massive influx of asylum-seeking immigrants have arrived, hoping to escape the repressive regimes and wars of Cuba, Iraq, Iran, Yugoslavia and Syria (to name a few).[174]

The changes have left their mark on the country. As of 2010, 14% of the population is foreign-born.[175] Immigrants compose approximately 15% of the working population but make up a larger percentage of the unemployed. As of 2013, Muslim immigrants accounted for approximately 6% of the population.[176]

---

173 https://www.bloomberg.com/news/articles/2019-01-31/swedish-liberalism-is-struggling-under-the-weight-of-immigration. Accessed 7/9/19.

174 https://www.cbsnews.com/news/sweden-rise-of-the-right-immigrants-unwelcome-cbsn-originals/. Accessed 7/9/19.

175 https://www.researchgate.net/figure/Foreign-born-people-Percentage-of-foreign-born-people-in-the-Swedish-population_fig1_233937522. Accessed 8/12/19.

176 http://www.wnd.com/2013/05/youth-rioting-in-sweden-its-the-muslims-stupid/. Accessed 10/20/15.

It is predicted that one million more immigrants will arrive within the next year, and eventually the white Swedish population may be the minority; incoming immigrants have a birth rate of about six times that of the Swedes.[177]

The Impact of Immigration

Swedes voted to keep the door open to an unsustainable flood of humanity and the country is now experiencing the inevitable results of its judgment-free, open-border policy.

With the influx of Muslim migrants, including many with ties to terrorist organizations, current statistics show that violent crime in Sweden has increased 300%.[178] In 1975, police records show a total of 421 rape cases. By 2014, the number had increased to 6,620, an increase of 1472%. Sweden is now number two in rape cases per capita, surpassed only by Lesotho, a tiny land-locked state in southern Africa. An increasing number of rapes are by Muslim males against non-Muslim females,[179] due to the huge influx of immigrants. In addition:

- Jews are fleeing Swedish cities due to the dangers of violent anti-Semitism

- Some schools are not only failing, they're also not safe for children

- Sweden has the fastest-growing income gap (think wage-inequality) in the world

- Free speech is being squelched

---

177 http://www.whyileftsweden.com/. Accessed 8/19/15.

178 http://www.gatestoneinstitute.org/5195/sweden-rape. Accessed 8/3/15.

179 http://www.sullivan-county.com/wcva/fjordman.htm. Accessed 10/20/15.

- Their economy is shrinking

- Segregation is rampant. [180]

How does a model nation join the Third World? Sweden may be on the path to finding out. Unlimited immigration of people who do not share the values of their adopted country can lead to "a cultural collapse."[181] Many Muslims believe they can do whatever they want and they won't be arrested, "in case it provokes them,"[182] leaving citizens with limited resources.

Sweden is the "canary in the coal mine," a portent of what could come. Democracy and free speech are viewed as principles to be punished. Anyone in Sweden who expresses the wrong opinion about Muslims is likely to be arrested—if the police are not busy running away from immigrant-incited violence.

Now, Sweden can look forward to an influx of more than 100,000 Muslim refugees who are escaping the civil war in Syria. A leading politician says Sweden is going to collapse because of the influx of Muslim refugees.[183]

One commentator says that Sweden deserves to see its culture destroyed because of their bad policies. But their children don't deserve this, and they are the ones who will pay the price.

"Sweden's not creating a utopia with its free and democratic welfare state," says Heath. "It's driving itself into oblivion."[184]

Sweden's current trajectory may be taking it precariously close to the socialist examples of earlier chapters. That would be a tragic outcome for

180 http://conservativepost.com/video-check-what-happened-to-this-country-that-accepted-more-immigrants-than-any-others/. Accessed 10/20/15.

181 Krystal Heath. "Sweden's Liberal Immigration Policies and Its Total Collapse…" http://louderwithcrowder.com/swedens-liberal-immigration-policies-and-its-total-collapse/. Accessed 8/3/15.

182 https://search.yahoo.com/yhs/search?p=muslims+won%27t+be+arrested+in+sweden+in+case+it+provokes+them&ei=UTF-8&hspart=mozilla&hsimp=yhs-001. Accessed 10/20/15.

183 https://www.rt.com/news/320158-sweden-refugees-collapse-catastrophe/. Accessed 10/30/15.

184 http://louderwithcrowder.com/swedens-liberal-immigration-policies-and-its-total-collapse/. Accessed 10/20/15.

a nation with strong roots in western civilization. It is that history—the roots of democracy—that we now turn to in order to understand the power of a free people.

5

DID ATHENS GET IT RIGHT?

Freedom, free enterprise, and the origins of democracy

**"Liberty is not a means to a higher political end.
It is itself the highest political end."**

--Lord Acton

From Cuba to Argentina and Venezuela, from Berlin to Greece and South Africa, even the most prosperous nations have paid a price for limiting—and losing—freedom. It is my argument, and history's record, that socialism fails fundamentally as an operating system for government.

The alternatives, of course, are also imperfect. By its very nature, any attempt to govern will always fall short. But there is one operating system that has the best track record, and that holds the most promise for the future as we aspire to move through Kahn's 400-year transition into continued and heightened prosperity. It's a system with a rich and storied history, one that has given us the most prosperous period in the entire span of humanity.

That system is a constitutional republic with democratically-elected representatives of the people.

It is generally accepted that the beginning of democracy took place in ancient Greece around 450 B.C. The Founding Fathers built many of the principles that govern our country on concepts of society and freedom in Ancient Greece and Rome. Some ancient Greek ideas, in turn, came from the monotheistic concepts of ancient Hebrews and Persian Zoroastrianism dating back as far as 3500 BC.

Democracy has been defined in various ways over time, and what people mean today by modern democracy looks quite different from its ancient origins. It is eye-opening to consider a 1928 U.S. War Department definition of democracy:

"A government of the masses. Authority derived through mass meeting or any other form of 'direct' expression. Results in mobocracy. Attitude toward property is communistic--negating property rights. Attitude toward law is that the will of the majority shall regulate, whether it be based upon deliberation or governed by passion, prejudice, and impulse, without restraint or regard to consequences. Results in demagogism, license, agitation, discontent, anarchy."[185]

By this definition, if there had been pure democracy in America in 2014, the angry mobs that flared up in Ferguson, Missouri, or during other riots, would have decided the law. In fact, Founding Fathers Alexander Hamilton and John Adams believed a constitutionally based republic was a far superior system to a pure democracy. Adams wrote that "there was never a democracy yet that did not commit suicide."[186]

The word "democracy" comes from the ancient Greek words for "rule of the people" (*demos* and *kratia*). Athenian Greek democracy represented the first system in world history in which assemblies of citizens who were technically equal before the law actually influenced the government. They were a democracy acting under laws they had given themselves.[187]

The critical word here, of course, is "technically." The Greeks had a fairly loose interpretation of democracy, and the system in ancient Greece was not the same as the one we enjoy today. The right to vote was granted to a "citizen," not a "person," and the two terms had some

---

185 http://www.freedom-school.com/freedom/democracy.htm. Accessed 8/11/15.

186 Brion McClanaham, PhD, *The Politically Incorrect Guide to the Founding Fathers*, Regnery Publishing, Washington, D.C., (2009), p. 11.

187 Professor J. Rufus Fears. The Great Courses, "History of Freedom." Lecture 1.

notable differences. Only adult males were "qualified to don togas, pop on pairs of sandals and mosey down to the weekly assemblies to cast their votes."[188] Citizenship was not offered to women, slaves, foreigners or males under 18. Women were only able to contract for small amounts of goods—all other decisions were made for them by the male head of the household.[189]

Still, Athenian democracy provided "group freedom," for lack of a better term, and it was an impressive innovation. In ancient Egypt around the same time, they didn't even have a word for freedom.[190]

In a modern democracy, elections are held to choose government officials. In the fourth century B.C., "drawing of lots" was used to select government officers. This was intended to allow all citizens to participate, and to avoid creating a professional governing class. Lots were selected from large groups of adult volunteers, and those chosen performed judicial, executive, and administrative functions. Decisions by these "lot" selections could even overrule the Assembly (similar to a Parliament or Legislature). [191]

When a jury was required, a group of 401 people served as jurors, selected at random from the populace. Since there were no police in Athens until the fifth century B.C., the jury brought charges as well as hearing the case, and they had extensive powers.[192] When a crime needed to be investigated, it was handled by the citizens themselves.[193]

The Greeks shared a common language, culture, and religion, yet they remained an independent people. They grouped into "city-states,"

---

188   http://history.howstuffworks.com/history-vs-myth/origins-democracy.htm. Accessed 4/8/14.

189   Blundell, Sue. *Women in ancient Greece, Volume 1995, Part 2*. Harvard University Press, 1995. At 115.

190   "History of Freedom." Lecture 1.

191   Bernard Manin. *Principles of Representative Government*. Cambridge: Cambridge University Press , 1997. At 19-23; https://en.wikipedia.org/wiki/Oligarchy - cite_note-7.

192   "History of Freedom." Lecture 2;
http://www.history.com/topics/ancient-history/ancient-greece-democracy.

193   http://greece.greekreporter.com/2013/05/30/the-police-in-ancient-greece/. Accessed 8/13/15.

each "an independently-run city with its own laws, customs, money and army,"[194] and they joined with other city-states when the need arose.

During the battle of Marathon[195] in 490 B.C., a small army of Greeks from various city-states outsmarted and prevailed against the huge Persian army. At the time, there was no democracy in Persia. The people were subservient to a totalitarian kingdom ruled by a monarch with absolute authority. And yet common men from the many independent Greek city-states were able to vanquish the proud and arrogant Persians.

Historians would say that the Greeks won because they were free men; fighting for their freedom is what motivated them to victory,[196] just as liberty was the motivation for the American Revolution.

And as for the "hubris" shown by the Persian king? The word ended up in Athenian law as a term meaning "rape."[197]

From Rome with Love: Individual Freedom Emerges

Under Alexander the Great, the ancient Greek king of Macedon, individual liberty began to flourish. Years later it received full acceptance under the ancient Roman Empire, and women and foreigners were finally given citizenship rights.[198] By 212 A.D., all freeborn Romans (both men and women) were considered citizens with equal rights. Freeborn Roman men wore togas as a sign of their freedom. The women wore stolas, a longer, dress-like garment, usually made of linen.[199]

With that liberty came a new freedom for commerce. Thought to be the first free-enterprise shopping center, Trajan's Market, was built

---

194 http://historylink101.com/2/greece3/city-state.htm. Accessed 8/12/15.

195 The modern "marathon," a run of 26 miles, came down to us from the ancient Greeks. Pheidippides (530-490 b.c.) was a long distance runner who ran the 26 mile distance from Marathon to Athens to warn the Athenians of the coming Persian invasion. After delivering the message, his heart burst and he dropped dead.

196 "History of Freedom." Lecture 1.

197 Id.

198 "History of Freedom." Lecture 2.

199 Until the 2nd century B.C., Roman women also wore togas, but after that time a woman wearing a toga was associated with prostitution.

by the Emperor Trajan in ancient Rome. It had multiple levels with 150 shops selling everything from food and clothing to spices. Likely constructed around 110-100 B.C., the ruins remain visible near the Coliseum to this day. [200]

Innovation blossomed during this free-market period. The ancient Romans invented central heating, warming their homes from beneath the floors. The homes of the rich had both heat and running water. Romans were the first civilization to skillfully use concrete and the arch in their architecture.

But it was not to last. The Roman *Republic* only lasted 125 years. The Roman *Empire* succeeded the Republic and lasted nearly 1500 years. The ideas that had made the Roman Republic great were progressively ignored by the Empire; individualism and entrepreneurialism were among the casualties. The great entrepreneurial advances of the Roman Republic were slowly overrun by more and more regulation. Gradually, businesses failed, taxes disappeared, provinces were stifled, government became oppressive, and the Empire collapsed.

The same thing is in danger of happening now.

The Debt We Owe The Brits: Magna Carta and Common Law

Individual liberty may have found its early footing with the Greeks and Romans, but it was in 1215 that freedom truly began to gain political traction upon the signing of a document in an open field in medieval England.

The document signed that day has been called "the most important bargain in the history of the human race."[201] King John issued the proclamation called the "Magna Carta" (Originally issued in Latin, its name means "great charter.") We know it best as the Magna Carta.

---

200   https://earlychurchhistory.org/food/trajans-market-ancient-romes-mall/. Accessed 9/19/19.

201   https://www.wsj.com/articles/magna-carta-eight-centuries-of-liberty-1432912022. Accessed 9/19/19.

King John issued the proclamation in response to a political crisis. The document's 63 provisions addressed grievances of the people and created certain rights, but the most important was the 39th clause:

> No free man shall be seized or imprisoned, or stripped of his rights or possessions, or outlawed or exiled, or deprived of his standing in any other way, nor will we proceed with force against him, or send others to do so, except by the lawful judgement of his equals or by the law of the land. To no one will we sell, to no one deny or delay, right or justice.[202]

That clause gave all "free men" the right to justice and a fair trial. It meant that everyone, including the King, was subject to the law—a groundbreaking idea at a time when monarchs held supreme power. In reality, the Magna Carta only affected a small group of men, the feudal barons. It left the peasants still at the mercy of their lords. But it was a start—the document is now considered to be the foundation for democracy in England, and a cornerstone of English liberties.

In the Magna Carta, freedom and property are "two expressions of the same principle."[203] The document ensured that one could keep goods without fear they would be confiscated by someone higher up the chain. It guaranteed that no free man could be arrested without due cause, nor could lands be attacked by the King at random. Even after the death of King John, the Magna Carta remained as the basis for the "rule of law" doctrine. As commonly understood, the "rule of law" means that all are subject to the same laws, an idea that was the source for vital legal

---

202 http://www.bl.uk/magna-carta/articles/magna-carta-an-introduction#sthash. lbv4vf47.dpuf. Accessed 11/19/15.

203 Daniel Hannan. "Magna Carta: Eight Centuries of Liberty." WSJ, The Saturday Essay. 5/29/15.

concepts of the American Constitution and Bill of Rights, including "no taxation without representation."[204]

Lord Alfred Thompson Denning (a populist judge who was known as a fighter for the underdog) called the Magna Carta "the greatest constitutional document of all times -- the foundation of the freedom of the individual against the arbitrary authority of the despot."

Denning felt that all the rights and privileges we enjoy today flowed from the proclamations of Magna Carta: "uncensored newspapers,[205] security of property, equality before the law, habeas corpus, regular elections, sanctity of contract, jury trials."

This is more than just Denning's opinion. At the time of the Constitutional Convention, the Founders of our country were well aware of the pitfalls involved in constructing a ruling document, and they looked to the Magna Carta for inspiration. The Founders "saw parliamentary government not as an expression of majority rule but as a guarantor of individual freedom."[206]

The year 2015 marked the 800th anniversary of The Magna Carta.[207] Only one monument to its creation remains in Britain. It was installed in the meadow in Surrey where the rascal King John placed his seal on the document.

It was placed there by the American Bar Association.[208]

A Country Founded on Ideals:
The "Operating System" of the United States of America
Imagine you were given the task of starting a new country from scratch.

---

204 http://www.crf-usa.org/foundations-of-our-constitution/magna-carta.html. Accessed 10/30/14.

205 In 2019 America, one might argue that newspapers can no longer be guaranteed to be "uncensored," given the rabid leftwing ideology of many journalists and publications.

206 Daniel Hannan. "Magna Carta: Eight Centuries of Liberty." WSJ, The Saturday Essay. 5/29/15.

207 Id.

208 *Id.*

What systems would you put in place? Who would you consult to decide the issues of the day? These are the challenges that faced America's Founding Fathers at the start of our constitutional republic.

The American Declaration of Independence was famously signed into law on July 4, 1776, signaling America's independence from the British.

> **"We hold these truths to be self-evident,**
> **that all men are created equal,**
> **that they are endowed by their Creator**
> **with certain unalienable rights;**
> **that among these are**
> **life, liberty, and the pursuit of happiness."**
>
> **--The Declaration of Independence,**
> **July 4, 1776**

But if the people were no longer subject to the British monarchy, what *were* they?

The Founders weren't quite sure what they were as a country, but they knew they weren't going to be subservient to a British king. Having come from a monarchy, they knew they didn't want another one. Instead, they wanted a free society where people could make their own decisions about how to live their lives, and where there were limitations on governmental involvement. As Plato said, change should come through agreement of the citizens. If there is no agreement, there is no right to impose it upon them.[209]

The Second Continental Congress issued a declaration in 1777 to the 13 newly-formed states that they should, "Adopt such a government as shall, in the opinion of the representatives of the people, best conduce to

---

209   Prof. J. Rufus Fears, The Great Courses, *A History of Freedom*, Disc 2.

the safety and happiness of their constituents in particular and America in general."[210]

Between 1777 and 1780, each of the 13 original states adopted a republican form of government—a government where political authority comes from the people. The word "republican" is taken from the ancient Roman Republic, and in its form, elected representatives are expected to transmit the will of the people to the government. The primary purpose of the Articles of Confederation, as they came to be called, was to allow the 13 states to deal with their defense and foreign policy. They also set down rules for the "operating system" that would guide the government.

It was felt, however, that the articles were too weak to allow effective government of an entire nation. In 1787, the Constitutional Convention gathered to lay out the plan for the form of a new government.

It was not an easy process.

During the Constitutional Convention[211] and the gatherings at Faneuil Hall in Boston, there were prolonged, vociferous arguments about whether the colonists should remain British subjects or be independent citizens of the new nation. It was in Faneuil Hall that citizens first protested the Sugar Act of 1764, crying "no taxation without representation."[212] This was a critical stepping-stone on the way to the American Revolution.

There was concern among the Founding Fathers about the risks of self-government. John Adams believed that history had shown that "the people could be just as oppressive as a king or an aristocracy;" he was in favor of a checked, balanced, separated form of government.

James Madison wryly and more succinctly observed, "If men were angels, no government would be necessary."[213]

---

210 Gordon Lloyd. "The Constitutional Convention." http://teachingamericanhistory.org/convention/intro/. Accessed 11/20/15.

211 The Constitutional Convention took place in Philadelphia, Pennsylvania, from May 25 to September 17, 1787.

212 http://www.faneuilhallboston.com/faneuilhallhistory/index.html. Accessed 10/22/14.

213 *The Federalist*, no. 51. The 51st of The Federalist Papers, which were originally published under a pseudonym, Publius.

Delegates to the Constitutional Convention did not believe "that a single unified nation as large as the United States could preserve its liberty."[214] Some spoke of "general" rather than "national" government. The delegates wanted to "empower a new government…while limiting those powers at the same time."

The Founders knew that most governments had been formed out of force or coercion, and they desperately wanted to avoid those traps. They understood that absolute power corrupted absolutely, and a free economy and respect for property rights were fundamental to assuring the freedom of individuals and the dispersion of power. They believed that the form of government they established would create, or significantly influence, the type of society that would develop.

As Madison observed, "In framing a government which is to be administered by men over men, the great difficulty lies in this: you must first enable the government to control the governed; and in the next place oblige it to control itself."[215]

David Mamet, the American playwright, offers his tongue-in-cheek assessment of what the Founders knew:

"The Constitution, written by men with some experience of actual government, assumes that the chief executive will work to be king, the Parliament will scheme to sell off the silverware, and the judiciary will consider itself Olympian and do everything it can to much improve (destroy) the work of the other two branches. So the Constitution pits them against each other, in the attempt not to achieve stasis, but rather to allow for the constant corrections necessary to prevent one branch from getting too much power for too long."[216]

Alexander Hamilton wanted to vest great power in the president. George Mason, however, feared that by conferring such power, "it may

---

214 http://www.faneuilhallboston.com/faneuilhallhistory/index.html. Accessed 10/22/14.

215 The Federalist Papers, no. 51. Published in Independent Journal, February 6, 1788.

216 *Why I am No Longer a Brain-Dead Liberal*, The Village Voice (NY), March 11, 2008. David Mamet was a lifelong liberal until his conversion to conservatism in 2008.

happen, at some future day, that he will establish a monarchy, and destroy the republic."[217]

Thomas Jefferson notably said: "My reading of history convinces me that most bad government results from too much government."[218]

Although most Americans wanted a republican form of government, there was no shortage of doubt about whether one could be constructed, and no clear consensus.

Fortunately for America, the yearning for freedom and the strong activist leadership of our founders carried the day. They prevailed with the help of those with a more neutral outlook, who were neither strongly for nor strongly against independence. After the heated debates in Faneuil Hall,[219] ultimately the "ayes" had it in favor of establishing a new and independent country.

The core group of Founders is generally considered to be George Washington, Thomas Jefferson, Samuel Adams, Benjamin Franklin, John Adams, John Hancock, James Madison, and Alexander Hamilton.[220]

The Founders had great expectations. Far from being a bunch of rich, white men trying to impose a system of government on a newly-created country,[221] they "drew on an astonishingly wide range of historical and

---

217 Debate in Virginia Ratifying Convention. http://press-pubs.uchicago.edu/ founders/ documents/a2_2_1s6.html. Accessed 8/11/15.

218 http://www.monticello.org/site/jefferson/bad-government-results-too-much-government-quotation. . Accessed 11/4/14.

219 Between 1764 and 1774, Faneuil Hall in Boston was the site of heated debates arguing against the taxes imposed by King George. Eventually, it was where the vote in favor of freedom was held. It was at Faneuil Hall, in August 1890, that one of the first Black legislators – Republican Julius Caesar Chappelle – argued for the right of Blacks to vote.

220 There were actually 238 individuals who could be considered founders, and 204 of them did one or more of the following:
Signed the Declaration of Independence
Signed the Articles of Confederation
Attended the Constitutional Convention of 1787
Signed the Constitution of the United States of America
Served as Senators in the First Federal Congress (1789-1791)
Served as U.S. Representatives in the First Federal Congress

221 The image portrayed in many history books today written by educators with a leftwing agenda.

philosophical sources and on a healthy skepticism of human nature to craft the most stable and free republic in world history."[222]

Each embraced strong moral principles, and without exception, they were highly accomplished and educated people with deep knowledge of the various forms of government going back to ancient times, including those of Ancient Greece, Ancient Rome, and the British Empire.

Thomas Jefferson, at the age of 33, was the primary drafter of the Declaration of Independence and the Statute of Virginia for Religious Freedom. He served as the third president of the United States. He had been a commissioner and then Minister to France (succeeding Benjamin Franklin), and at the age of 76 he founded the University of Virginia, spearheading the legislative campaign for its charter, securing the location, and designing the university buildings. He also planned its curriculum and served as the first rector.[223]

Jefferson's collection of books constituted the nucleus of the Library of Congress at its inception. He thought it vital for all students to study political history and foreign affairs in order "to give an understanding of the virtues of republican representative democracy, the dangers that threatened it, and the responsibility of its citizens to esteem and protect it. This education was to be a common experience for all citizens, rich and poor, for every one of them had natural rights and powers, and every one had to understand and esteem the institutions, laws and traditions of his country if it was to succeed."[224]

Ben Franklin had a difficult childhood and ended up running away from home. He got into printing and eventually purchased *The Pennsylvania Gazette*. In *Poor Richard's Almanac*, he authored many famous phrases, including "A penny saved is a penny earned." In the 1730s and 40s, he was involved in the campaign to "clean, pave and light Philadelphia's streets."[225]

---

222   https://www.prageru.com/video/who-killed-the-liberal-arts. Accessed 11/30/15.

223   http://www.biography.com/people/thomas-jefferson-9353715#early-life. Accessed 11/30/15.

224   Donald Kagan.   "Democracy Requires a Patriotic Education."   Wall Street Journal, Opinion. 6/26/14.   http://www.wsj.com/articles/donald-kagan-democracy-requires-a-patriotic-education-1411770193?mg=id-wsj. Accessed 9/27/14; 8/11/15.

225   http://www.ushistory.org/franklin/info/index.htm. Accessed 11/30/15.

Among his other accomplishments, Franklin helped found The Library Company (the first subscription book lending company in America), the American Philosophical Society, and the Philadelphia Hospital. He also helped launch the first firefighter company in Philadelphia, and one of the first insurance companies.

Franklin invented swim fins, the glass harmonica, and bifocals. His experiments showing the nature and the power of electricity earned him international fame.

He spent time in England but came back to America after a disagreement with the British Foreign ministry. He then began his work toward an independent nation. After signing the Declaration of Independence, he sailed to France as an ambassador to the court of Louis XVI.

Due mostly to Franklin's pleasing personality, the French signed a Treaty of Alliance, and in 1783 signed the Treaty of Paris, after the Americans won the revolution. Franklin returned to the States, participated in the Constitutional Convention, signed the Constitution, and prior to his death wrote an anti-slavery treatise.

Many feel that the Founding Fathers are only a distant, historical note— too far in the past and no longer relevant to the issues of today. But had it not been for them, we might still be a colony in the British Empire. We take America for granted, but to create it they put everything on the line—"...our lives, our fortunes and our sacred honor... ,"[226] so that we could have a country and live in freedom.

It was a venture that included great personal danger. As Franklin said, "we must all hang together or, most assuredly, we will hang separately."

A Constitutional Republic Is The Best System
With all their knowledge, experience, and high standards, the Founders considered all forms of government, and settled on a constitutional republic as the best system.

---

226 Declaration of Independence, 7/4/1776.

There were 55 delegates to the Constitutional Convention and 39 signed the finished document. The Constitution of the United States was signed in 1788 by 11 of the 13 states (9 state ratifications were required for passage; Virginia and Massachusetts declined).[227] This vote, with only two votes to spare for ratification, helps put into perspective the decision to pass on the slavery issue.

The vote for ratification was very close, and ratification required support from some of the southern states. They would not have voted in favor if the slavery issue had not been handled the way it was. There is no way the Constitution would have been ratified if slavery had been addressed at that time, and the United States would not have come into existence.

Tragically, but necessarily, the United States would fight its bloodiest war in history to end slavery a very long 73 years later.

Upon leaving the Constitutional Convention on its final day, a woman asked Benjamin Franklin, "Well, Doctor, what have we got? A republic or a monarchy?" To which Franklin replied, "A republic, if you can keep it."[228]

Franklin's answer epitomized the views of all the Founders. In the course of designing the Constitution, they had systematically studied the experience of governments and nations throughout history. They were under no illusions that their solutions would be without challenges. They knew that the political system they had created was fragile, but hoped that their creation could resist the forces that would periodically confront it.

The new government under the U.S. Constitution became operational on March 4, 1789.

Regrettably, some liberal administrators are attempting to rewrite history, even writing the Founders out of the history books. Writing

---

227 Among the objections were that the Constitutional Convention had exceeded its authority in convening, that the document didn't represent everyone's interests, and the most serious objection was that the Convention had failed to adopt a Bill of Rights. This was remedied by the promise that the first task of the new government would be to do so.

228 Charles Murray. American Exceptionalism: An Experiment in History. At 48.

for the American Thinker, Patrick Jakeway relates that in 2014, The College Board[229] removed all reference to the founding fathers from their educational materials, with the exception of a brief reference to George Washington's final address.[230] They labeled the New World as "a racist, genocidal, imperialist nation."[231]

This view completely distorts history. If it weren't for the wisdom of the Founding Fathers, we wouldn't have a country.

"If your child never learns about Benjamin Franklin's story or about how the Revolutionary War was won or about the Gettysburg Address or about the D-Day landing at Normandy (all erased in this 'brave new history'), then he will never know that it is up to us to keep our Republic. It is for us the living never to forget our forefathers, who fought and sacrificed for us that we might live a life of liberty. It is for us to be dedicated here to the unfinished work they so nobly advanced."[232]

Donald Kagan comments that America cannot rely on a common ancestry and tradition, as did so many other societies. Instead, we must rely on common ideas— the ideas that formed our Constitution. We are an enormously diverse and varied people. We are a country of immigrants, but it is important to remember that our ancestors were *legal* immigrants. "Every country requires a high degree of cooperation and unity among its citizens if it is to achieve the internal harmony that every good society requires."[233]

How can such a unity be achieved if its citizens are ignorant of the history behind its traditions and the policies resulting therefrom?

---

229 The College Board publishes the SAT (Scholastic Aptitude Test) and the AP exam. They are a Los Angeles-based not for profit organization offering learning and networking opportunities for educators and students.

230 Patrick Janeway. "College Board Erases the Founding Fathers." *American Thinker* magazine. Aug. 16, 2014. http://www.americanthinker.com/articles/2014/08/college_board_erases_the_founding_fathers_protect_the_spirit_of_76.html. Accessed 8/10/15.

231 Id.

232 College Board Erases the Founders. Education News. 8/16/14. http://www.educationviews.org/college-board-erases-the-founding-fathers/. Accessed 12/4/15.

233 https://www.wsj.com/articles/donald-kagan-democracy-requires-a-patriotic-education-1411770193. Accessed 9/20/19.

240 Years and Counting

Our founders learned from the Greeks, the Romans and the Magna Carta, but they didn't stop there. The new government was to be a constitutionally based republic that would allow maximum freedoms and flexibility, while avoiding the problems the Greeks had with pure democracy. Most critically, there would be checks and balances on all branches of government including on those the people elected to represent them.

Yes, government might be slow and cumbersome, but there would be protections against potentially tyrannical authoritarians—both individuals or an impetuous majority. Mostly, it has worked. Our founders were serious, learned, dedicated and brilliant leaders. Best of all, the system they framed for us has continued to attract good people to service for nearly two and a half centuries. Though quality and results have been mixed, we can be mostly grateful for our leaders through this period.

My familiarity with grassroots politics started when I was about 8 years old. My mother, a precinct committeewoman, gave me a nickel ($.05) to pass out sample ballots throughout the precinct. Though perhaps overpaid, it started my appreciation for the profit motive. For over seventy years, I have come to know many politicians, and was even a member of that group myself for four years as city councilman for all of Denver. Of the hundreds of politicians I have known through the years, most are well above average, bright, well-educated, balanced, dedicated and public-spirited. They tend to be focused on their constituents' wishes while understanding they can't please everyone all the time and that there are almost always two sides to every public issue. Some have simply been outstanding individuals and leaders.

I believe it is lazy thinking to scorn all politicians. When we condemn them as a group, we are really condemning the system our founders set up. Rather than categorically condemn ruling elites, the faction that has bad ideas should be identified and condemned. If leftist authoritarian elites or some other groups are the problem, they should be singled out for what they are rather than condemning all public servants. All elected representatives should be criticized when they are out of line, but

usually, they should be given the benefit of the doubt—that at least most of their motives are good.

In his futuristic novel set in a totalitarian State, author George Orwell opined:

"The most effective way to destroy people is to deny and obliterate their own understanding of their history."[234]

Make it a priority to incorporate the founding of America into your education (and that of your children), even if you have to buy the books yourself or get the information online. How else can you or your children gain a true understanding of the origins of freedom and what it means to live in a free society?

Individual liberty, individual responsibility, pluralism: those are the fundamentals of our country. Are those ideas ever going to be out of date? Not as long as people have the opportunity to experience them.

Our Constitution and Bill of Rights are similar to a computer's operating system. Without an operating system for a computer, no flood of data can be organized to produce useful output. Without an operating system for a country, there is no structure for the rules of a free society.

Once you create the operating system, it can be duplicated almost without additional cost anywhere around the world. We are the most admired and envied people on the planet, as evidenced by the desire to immigrate here. Unfortunately, few governments have adopted our ideals, and that is one of the reasons for today's immigration problems.

In his "I have a dream" speech, Martin Luther King referred to "the magnificent words of the Constitution and Declaration of Independence."[235] Like King, we should be proud of ourselves and our heritage, and not reluctant to advocate our founding ideals. Yet, we seem to be drifting to the opposite direction.

In a bizarre incident, during a trip to Egypt, U.S. Supreme Court Justice Ruth Bader Ginsburg recommended that Egypt adopt the Canadian or South African constitution, but not that of the United

---

234 http://www.goodreads.com/author/quotes/3706.George_Orwell. Accessed 8/2/15.
235 http://www.archives.gov/press/exhibits/dream-speech.pdf. Accessed 9/12/14.

States—the very constitution that justices swear to uphold and defend.[236]

As U.S. President Ronald Reagan said, "Freedom is not free." Effort and dedication are required to maintain a free society. That effort, notes Founding Father Samuel Adams, takes not a majority, but "an irate, tireless minority, keen on setting brushfires of freedom in the minds of men."[237]

Charles Krauthammer observed that America offers liberty, not equality. In other words, the Founders acknowledged that a happy life can only be created by each of us, individually. The Statue of Liberty is not called the "Statue of Equality" for good reason. Under the constitution, we all have the right to the *pursuit* of happiness, but a guarantee of happiness cannot be bestowed by government. Each person must develop his particular life, and pursue happiness according to his own values, ambitions, and efforts.

This is the essence of individualism. By contrast, socialism is state-controlled collectivism. It aims to establish a government monopoly based on control of the economy and property. That kind of system would destroy our founding ideals.

"The aim of socialism," says Friedrich Hayek, "is no less than to effect a complete redesigning of our traditional morals, law, and language, and ... to stamp out the old order..."[238]

Stamping out "the old order" is one of the longstanding battle cries of the Left. They want to change everything in America that has worked pretty well for over 240 years, into something that has failed nearly everywhere it's been tried.

When Barack Obama said in 2008 that he was going to bring "fundamental change" to the United States, I wonder how many thought that what he meant was to turn America into a social welfare State.

---

236 https://www.dailysignal.com/2012/02/08/justice-ginsburg-i-would-not-look-to-the-u-s-constitution/. Accessed 9/19/19.

237 https://madisonliberty.org/brushfires. Accessed 9/20/19.

238 *The Fatal Conceit.* Chicago: University of Chicago Press, 1988. At 67.

Controversial preacher and community activist Al Sharpton declared: "The American public overwhelmingly voted for socialism when they voted for Barack Obama."[239]

Did they? I'll bet that statement came as a big surprise to many Obama voters. Who really understood what Obama meant by "fundamental change"?

What have we seen in America with this "fundamental change"? In the period of 2008 to 2016, the number of food stamp recipients greatly increased and the number of those *not* in the working force increased to 95 million. Many businesses went bust, and banks and car manufacturers were bailed out with taxpayer money.

Historically, this isn't the kind of change that has improved the living standards of our country.

Unfortunately, with the ideas of Bernie Sanders and the radical Leftists in Congress, the country would go headlong into socialism.

Property Rights are a Hallmark of a Free Society.

From Greece to Rome, from England to the United States, a pattern emerges: Increasing the freedom of a society increases its ability to prosper.

As Friedrich Hayek points out, however, property rights and their enforcement are a central element of this equation. "Property rights" means that you have the right to accumulate property (money, goods, real estate) and to do with it as you wish—including the right to *keep* it. That right is protected by the *rule of law*, a commitment to a system in which just laws are enacted that safeguard your right to work in free enterprise and to retain the fruits of your labor and property. There are those who would enhance their own wealth and power by taking yours. Property rights, enforced by law, protect you.

---

239   March 22, 2010. https://ayfs.wordpress.com/2010/03/22/al-sharpton-the-american-public-overwhelmingly-voted-for-socialism-when-they-elected-president-obama/. Accessed 8/5/15.

Freedom of economic activity does mean freedom *under the law*, but not freedom from *all* government restraint. The challenge is that restricting property rights has historically led to repression. The Heritage Foundation created a chart that articulates how freedom decreases in direct proportion to the loss of property rights:

- **100%**—Private property is guaranteed by the government. The court system enforces contracts efficiently and quickly. The justice system punishes those who unlawfully confiscate private property. There is no corruption or expropriation.

- **90**—Private property is guaranteed by the government. The court system enforces contracts efficiently. The justice system punishes those who unlawfully confiscate private property. Corruption is nearly nonexistent, and expropriation is highly unlikely.

- **80**—Private property is guaranteed by the government. The court system enforces contracts efficiently but with some delays. Corruption is minimal, and expropriation is highly unlikely.

- **70**—Private property is guaranteed by the government. The court system is subject to delays and is lax in enforcing contracts. Corruption is possible but rare, and expropriation is unlikely.

- **60**—Enforcement of property rights is lax and subject to delays. Corruption is possible but rare, and the judiciary may be influenced by other branches of government. Expropriation is unlikely.

- **50**—The court system is inefficient and subject to delays. Corruption may be present, and the judiciary may be influenced by other branches of government. Expropriation is possible but rare.

- **40**—The court system is highly inefficient, and delays are so long that they deter the use of the court system. Corruption is present, and the judiciary is influenced by other branches of government. Expropriation is possible.

- **30**—Property ownership is weakly protected. The court system is highly inefficient. Corruption is extensive, and the judiciary is strongly influenced by other branches of government. Expropriation is possible.

- **20**—Private property is weakly protected. The court system is so inefficient and corrupt that outside settlement and arbitration is the norm. Property rights are difficult to enforce. Judicial corruption is extensive. Expropriation is common.

- **10**—Private property is rarely protected, and almost all property belongs to the state. The country is in such chaos (for example, because of ongoing war) that protection of property is almost impossible to enforce. The judiciary is so corrupt that property is not protected effectively. Expropriation is common.

> - **0%**—Private property is outlawed, and all property belongs to the state. People do not have the right to sue others and do not have access to the courts. Corruption is endemic.

Milton Friedman, one of the greatest economists of our time, singles out Hong Kong as an example of the economic surge that can take place where free enterprise abounds.

Once a tiny colonial backwater with a per capita income of about one-fourth that of Great Britain, one British Lord stated in 1844 that "There does not appear the slightest probability that, under any circumstances, Hong Kong will ever become a place of trade." [240]

At the time, Britain— the birthplace of the Industrial Revolution— was a 19th century superpower. Hong Kong, meanwhile, had little more to offer than its expansive harbor.

Yet by 1996, the average individual income in Hong Kong had grown to be one-third larger than the average in Great Britain.[241]

How did this happen? The answer lies in the choice of operating systems: Hong Kong chose freedom.

After World War II, the two countries varied greatly in their strategies. Great Britain went the way of socialism: taxes, regulations and an anti-business environment. Hong Kong, by contrast, was governed by a disciple of Adam Smith[242] who believed in *laissez-faire* free markets "with

240   Andrew P. Moriss. "Freedom Works: The case of Hong Kong. Freedom from Regulation Promotes Prosperity." 11/1/08. http://fee.org/freeman/freedom-works-the-case-of-hong-kong/. Accessed 9/19/19.

241   GSB/Chicago: *The Real Lesson of Hong Kong.* www.chicagobooth.edu/magazine/fall97/hongkong. html. Accessed 10/13/14.

242   One of the founders of classical free market economic theory, author of the first comprehensive book on economics, *The Wealth of Nations.* "Wealth" in this context referred to the general well-being of a nation.

no tariffs and low taxes."[243] Colonists had the freedom to contract. They held property rights and there were laws to protect those rights.

And so it was that England began its road to relative decline, and Hong Kong began its road to prosperity.

Henry Hazlett, author of "Economics in One Lesson," relates that in 1979 the British government was taxing personal income up to 83%, and investment income up to 98%. "Should it be surprising" he says, "that it has discouraged work and investments and so profoundly discouraged production and employment? There is no more certain way to deter employment than to harass and penalize employers."[244]

As Jack Kemp said, "You can't create new employees without creating new employers."[245]

The story of these two economies is a picture-perfect demonstration of which system works best. Free enterprise comes out on top.

However, in Hong Kong, the siege for greater control by Beijing that began in 2019 could change their situation.

———

We have arrived at the inescapable conclusion that socialism is much like a house of cards. Even Karl Marx could not provide a workable structure upon which to hang his sugarcoated concepts. His long, obscure musings are only theories, repeated and expanded upon by silver-tongued politicians. In the real world, those theories simply do not work.

The reason Marx's ideas were fundamentally flawed was that he focused on the division of wealth rather than its creation. Unfortunately, some extreme environmental ideas carry along the perceptions of the

243   GSB Chicago. *The Real Lesson of Hong Kong.* http://0055d26.netsolhost.com/friedman/pdfs/other_av/MFlecture.05.14.1997.pdf . Accessed 8/7/15; http://www.chicagobooth.edu/magazine/fall97/hongkong.html. Accessed 10/7/14.

244   *Economics in One Lesson.*" NY: Three Rivers Press (Crown Publishing/Random House), 1979. At 206.

245   Jack Kemp was a professional football player, and Secretary of Housing and Urban Development from 1989-1993.

limits of growth. The developments of the information and communications revolutions, propelled by the realities of Moore's law, suggest this thinking is out of date. By contrast Kahn's "great transition" thinking assumes no limits to growth. Is such an assumption real world?

Kahn looked seriously at all energy sources and potentials and all natural resources. He believed, and events are proving, that Paul Ehrlich and other modern day Malthusians ignored the market factor: That when prices for commodities go up, more is produced or less expensive substitutes are found. Copper is a good example. Plastic pipes have displaced copper tubes in countless applications. Not only does plastic tend to last longer, it costs less.

Kahn also believed world potentials for energy were plentiful and increasing. Solar power was in its infancy but is now competitive and growing steadily. Same for wind. Hydrocarbon sources continue to expand most recently with the U.S. boom in fracking technology. Nuclear essentially has unlimited potential if we continue to develop the new nuclear technologies at hand—both advanced fission and fusion. Advanced nuclear *fission* will be dramatically safer, be substantially less expensive, have less potential for proliferation, and eliminate nuclear waste as a significant issue. Nuclear *fusion*, the energy of our sun, is being duplicated on earth. It is still a few decades away from being economically competitive, but it promises the world virtually unlimited energy for billions of years.

An international consortium including the U.S., Europe, Japan, Russia, China, S. Korea, India and several other countries, is nearing completion of a new Magnetic Confinement Fusion facility in France that will produce more energy than it consumes and pave the way to development of commercial units. This consortium, ITER (International Thermonuclear Experimental Reactor) represents the best in international cooperation. Advanced fission and fusion represent the ultimate in clean energy. There are no emissions except minimal waste heat.

Energy can also deal with water shortages. There is plenty of water in the world. About 70% of the earth is covered by it. Problem is, it is too salty for most usages. Energy and science have made water desalination realtively economical through reverse osmosis (RO). God invented RO, but General Atomics was an early inventor of *membranes* that made it practical through research in the 1960's and 1970's. Since then there have been major improvements in the technology requiring less electrical energy to push saline water through RO membranes.

Even new technologies for growing and harvesting algae represent potentials for virtually unlimited clean energy at a reasonable cost. And, if the potential for unlimited energy doesn't make you feel good about the future, algae can also represent a virtually unlimited source of protein for feeding fish, cattle, chickens and humans.

Our little company has done major research with DARPA (Defense Advanced Research Projects Agency) on Algae and has been a pioneer in Advanced fission and fusion for nearly sixty years. The persistence, dedication and hard work by smart people, stimulated by the U.S. Department of Energy, is starting to pay off for the promise of unlimited energy and productivity that will be possible throughout the world.

The potentials for unlimited energy are being supercharged by the quantum effects of Moore's law on the information, communications and artificial intelligence revolutions. The combination of technologies, free people and free enterprise are showing that Marx completely missed the most dynamic factors for human progress. Wherever his ideas have been tried, they have eventually caused regression and misery.

The late Margaret Thatcher, former British Prime Minister, visited communist countries and observed that "... their politicians never hesitate to boast about their achievements. They know them all by heart; they reel off the facts and figures, claiming this is the rich harvest of the Communist system. Yet they are not prosperous as we in the West are prosperous, and they are not free as we in the West are free."[246]

---

246 First speech as Leader of Conservative Party. http://www.margaretthatcher.org/speeches.

Americans experience the Soviet Union

In 1971, I was lucky to be selected one of twelve "Young Political Leaders" for an unprecedented eighteen-day visit to the Soviet Union. We were hosted by "young Soviet political leaders" from Moscow, Leningrad, Samarkand, Tashkent, Kiev and Novosibirsk.

We were allowed to see things that few Americans had seen up to that time. We also went toe to toe with them in debates about the relative merits of our political systems. Pat Buchanan, then a young speech writer for President Richard M. Nixon, usually led the rhetorical charge from our side. I think we opened some young Soviet political leaders' eyes.

Aside from too little sleep and too many Vodka toasts, it was a great opportunity to see the Soviet Union up close and personal.

Similar to my experience in the Soviet Union in 1971, a friend's son from Southern California went to Soviet Russia as an exchange student in the 1960s. He and his classmates were harangued over the six weeks with propaganda about the "utopia" of the communist system. They were taken on local outings where they observed the best that Russia had to offer—but always in the company of guides and under strict supervision.

They were all aware that they were only being shown locations approved by the government, not the areas where normal Russians lived. Even so, everything they were shown was greatly inferior in comfort and style to their American environment. Their guides, of course, would have had no idea; they had no access to a free press and knew very little about the outside world.

After the class series was over, the Russian teacher took a few of the group members aside. She told them they were not being recorded and could talk openly.[247] Then she asked them, "How many of you have your own car?" All of them were over 16 (the driving age in most of America at that time) and they all raised their hand. "How many of you live in your own private house?" They all raised their hand. "How many of you can shop anywhere you want?" They all raised their hand.

---

247 An admission that they probably *were* being recorded at other times in their tour.

The result of this exchange was that the teacher became so furious she wouldn't speak further with them. She was absolutely convinced that they were giving her the propaganda of the American government. She could not possibly conceive of them telling the truth, because at that time in history (before smartphones and the internet) Russians were only shown photos of slums and ghettos in America, and very little truth filtered down to them from outside sources.

The teacher did not believe it possible that all of them had houses and cars, or that they could shop in stores frequented by the elite. Her incredulity was probably bolstered by the fact that she knew the propaganda she was forced to teach in her classroom was not a truthful portrayal of Russian life. It was no great leap for her to imagine that the American students were also required by their government to propagate falsehoods.

As soon as the internet and smartphones became universally available, the Russian government was at a loss to stop their citizens from viewing and participating in the modern world. The ensuing prosperity evolved only because restrictions on elementary capitalism were lifted, at least for some.

Even today, many companies are granted privileges because they support the regime in power. That regime still wields a strong hand in controlling the Russian people.

How Much Government is Enough?

Choosing the right operating system isn't the end of the path to a free and prosperous society. Even in a free nation governed by its people, the operating system itself can become unwieldy, and threaten to consume the liberty it was intended to preserve. There is constant pressure to provide more services. This must be balanced by the knowledge that payment for government services must come (and only comes) from payment by hard working taxpayers.

Friedrich Hayek believed that government should only manage those elements of society that no one else could manage, such as defense. He thought just about everything should be privatized, from "education to transport and communications, including post, telegraph, telephone and broadcasting services, all the so-called 'public utilities,' the various 'social' insurances and, above all, the issue of money."[248]

In 1834, William Leggett, a Jacksonian Democrat and abolitionist, had an even stricter view, and believed that government should be strictly limited to "the protection of person and property from domestic and foreign enemies."[249]

In contrast, regulation is a key component of a socialist society; it's how the government gains and retains power. Under the Barack Obama administration[250] in America, thousands of pages of regulations were passed, dumping ever more restrictions on individuals and small businesses. Many businesses failed due to over-regulation.

As Ronald Reagan said "The nine most terrifying words in the English language are, 'I'm from the government and I'm here to help.'"

Prominent economist Milton Friedman comments on a "general rule" of excessive government:

"If a private enterprise is a failure, it closes down— unless it can get a government subsidy to keep it going; if a government enterprise fails, it is expanded. I challenge you to find exceptions." [251]

Friedman uses the example of the International Monetary Fund (the IMF), which was formed to help countries affected by World War II by administering a system of fixed exchange rates. When the fixed exchange rate was eliminated in 1971, the IMF was not shut down. Instead, in typical public sector style, it changed its function to "helping" developing nations.

It went further than that....

---

248 Wapshott, Nicholas. *Keynes/Hayek: The Clash That Defined Modern Economics.* New York: W.W. Norton, 2011. At 291.

249 http://oll.libertyfund.org/quotes/340. Accessed 11/3/15.

250 2008-2016.

251 Bill Flax. "The Credit Crunch is Washington's Creation." Real Clear Markets. 10/27/09. http://www.realclearmarkets.com/articles/2009/10/27/the_credit_crunch_is_washingtons_creation_97471.html. Accessed 10/27/15.

During the Bretton Woods conference, two agencies were created, one to promote development, one to administer fixed rates. Thus government grew again and, according to Friedman, both of the agencies have done more harm than good.

The better move would have been to limit the IMF to its original purpose of encouraging international financial stability and exchange rate. But agencies like the IMF develop their own constituencies and do what they can to perpetuate the system. As Friedman says:

> "The general rule is that government undertakes an activity that seems desirable at the time. Once the activity begins, whether it proves desirable or not, people in both the government and the private sector acquire a vested interest in it. If the initial reason for undertaking the activity disappears, they have a strong incentive to find another justification for its continued existence." [252]

The United States Department of Commerce, for example, purportedly works "to promote job creation, economic growth, sustainable development, and improved standards of living for Americans." Isn't that what free enterprise does? If you leave the free market the space to work, it regulates itself—it is self-correcting. In free markets, free people work, produce and trade in mutually agreeable ways. When those ways aren't mutually agreeable, free people work and trade elsewhere with others.

The foundation of free markets are free people with the freedom to choose with whom and how they wish to do business. Government bureaucracies, monopolies with the power of coercion, make those decisions in socialistic economies.

The Department of Energy's number one responsibility is to look after our nuclear laboratories and nuclear weapons. It is an agency that cannot be privatized.

---

252 *Why Government Is the Problem*. Stanford University: Hoover Essay, Hoover Institution on War, Revolution and Peace, 1993. At 9.

But to ensure that the nation has low-cost energy, private utility companies can do a better job than government. They can provide the networks and the generating capacity, and they are competitive so they keep the price of electricity down. It would be better to have minimal interference from government in selecting energy technologies, and leave energy production in the hands of the private sector and the market.

The Veteran's Administration is run badly. If it were privatized, veterans could be given vouchers for treatment at the hospital of their choosing. They give life and limb for their country; we should make all healthcare options open to them when they come home. The Trump Administration is working toward those goals, but there is still much to be done.

The federal Department of Education could be drastically reduced. Education at all levels should be primarily under state or local control. Local entities are more knowledgeable about the needs of their residents. Competition in education will determine what stimulates progress. In the internet age, that should include the potential for better-utilizing computers in the classroom.

The closer to the problem an organization is, the better the solution it can find. Local government (as long as it is politically neutral) is much better at determining the education needed for its residents. National government should only be involved if there is an issue that can't be dealt with at the local level. Leaving tax dollars where they are generated, and keeping them under local control, is a good start.

Unfortunately, as the comedian and satirist George Carlin said, "Governments don't want a population capable of critical thinking. They want obedient workers, people just smart enough to run the machines, and just dumb enough to passively accept their situation."[253]

Winston Churchill claimed that "When one has reached the summit of power and surmounted so many obstacles, there is a danger of becoming convinced that one can do anything one likes and that any strong

---

253 http://boardofwisdom.com/togo/Quotes/ShowQuote?msgid=559371#.VFd_FRZxiZQ. Accessed 11/3/14.

personal view is necessarily acceptable to the nation and can be enforced upon one's subordinates."[254]

We are seeing too much of this, particularly in the period 2010 to 2016, as the executive branch of government made laws through executive fiat and rules that were contrary to what best serves the public. Matt Ridley reminds us that, because government is a monopoly, a greater threat comes from government than from "market failure." Government "brings inefficiency and stagnation to most things it runs."[255]

Yet despite that inefficiency, he notes that "most clever people still call for government to run more things and assume that if it did so, it would somehow be more perfect, more selfless, next time."[256]

What was it Einstein said? "The definition of insanity is doing the same thing over and over again and expecting different results."[257] Samuel Johnson made a comment about multiple marriages that also applies to regulation: "It represents the triumph of hope over experience."[258]

Peter H. Schuck concludes that "the endemic failure [of public policy decisions] is a consequence of the nature of modern government."[259] Schuck argues that to be successful, "a public policy has to get six things right: incentives, instruments, information, adaptability, credibility and management. The federal government tends to be bad at all of these."

He uses the example of Medicare, a popular program, defining it as the imposition of "a mid-1960s insurance model" that is inflexible, creates shortages, abides billions in fraud and invites "waste and abuse."[260]

254　*The Wit and Wisdom of Winston Churchill*. At 75.

255　Matt Ridley. *The Rational Optimist*. UK: Harper Collins, 2011.

256　Id.

257　http://eaglerising.com/1912/democrats-run-americas-ten-poorest-cities/#hShcJYegQTx9dzQo.99. Accessed 8/16/15.

258　John Tamny. *Popular Economics*. Washington, D.C.: Regnery Publishing, 2015. At 105.

259　Book Review: Yual Levin, reviewing Peter H. Schuck, 'Why Government Fails so Often," Wall Street Journal, Bookshelf, June 9, 2014.

260　Id.

Schuck strikes at the heart of the liberal political platform by finding that "[t]heir worldview depends on a degree of government competence that is simply unattainable."[261]

You can look at the examples in your own community to verify the inefficiency of the public sector. If you have to choose a hospital for a critical health problem, would you rather go to your County hospital or to the Mayo Clinic? When you walk into the post office, are you pleased with the bland and sometimes rundown facility? What about the service of the employees? Why do so many businesses ship through UPS or FedEx rather than the post office? It's because they know that the privately run business gives better service, and that (with exceptions) the employees have a better attitude because working for private industry is more rewarding. Employees in the private sector know it is the customer that provides the money that pays their salaries.

Conservatives tend to believe in working for a living, making jobs and being productive. Many liberals are more inclined to expect entitlements for themselves and their constituents as a life plan. The entitlement mentality is at odds with the essential need for productivity.

It is a serious problem for our country, especially given the influx of illegal immigrants. Once you give something for free, it's hard to take it back. It may be given as a temporary fix, but it rarely goes away. As Ronald Reagan said in his first inaugural address as President of the United States: "Government is not the solution to the problem. Government *is* the problem."[262]

The Obama administration seemed to use the European model of entitlement, regulation and income redistribution as their guide. It may be one of the few examples in history when a structurally flawed and deficient system was being used as a model for success. Like any entity, government has a strong incentive to grow and perpetuate itself.

---

261   Id.
262   January 20, 1981.

In a discussion with "Joe the Plumber"[263] in 2008 on the campaign trail, Obama famously said that he thought redistribution was a good thing. "[W]hen you spread the wealth around, it's good for everybody," said Obama. What Obama failed to understand is that free markets and free enterprise create wealth and are far better at spreading it around than governments.

Even conservative politicians who believe in less government spending find it hard to vote for programs that lessen their own authority and power. It has been said that government's inclination is to tax anything that moves, regulate anything that grows, and subsidize anything that stops moving. Our Founders knew that and tried to limit that insidious infection.

One Harvard Economics professor believes that fiscal stimulus just doesn't work.[264]

Large financial programs should be undertaken only if they can be individually justified in economic terms.

Social Security was initiated originally to assist the elderly who had a 50% poverty rate during the Depression. It's still here today, though predictions are that the system will be bankrupt within the next 50 years or so. To some extent, Social Security is a Ponzi scheme – taking from some to give to others while not being able to maintain an adequate reserve to back up future promises.

At the beginning of Social Security, it was estimated there were twelve workers paying into the program for every retiree receiving benefits. Now the ratio is closer to three to one. The program is unsustainable and adjustments must be made.

The Texas model is probably a good one to follow. In the 1980s, three counties (Galveston, Matagorda, Brazoria) opted out of Social Security and instead privately invested the funds. Top-rated financial institutions

263 Samuel Joseph Wurzelbacher, known as Joe the Plumber, is an American conservative activist and commentator.

264 http://www.telegraph.co.uk/finance/economics/8618623/Fiscal-stimulus-doesnt-work-claims-Harvard-economics-professor-Robert-Barro.html. Accessed 8/16/15.

bid for the money, and over the years retirees have earned between 3.75 – 5.75%, which increased at times to 7% during the 1990s. The plan also includes a death benefit, survivor's insurance, and a term life insurance plan. In 2011, a middle income worker making $51,200/yearly would see a benefit of $3,600/monthly, compared to $1,540 under Social Security.

Why don't more counties and states go this way? Because "progressive" politicians have convinced their voters that they aren't smart enough to take care of themselves but need the government to do it for them. The facts prove otherwise.

I believe in the inherent good judgment of the American people

At a minimum, the age requirement for Social Security should be increased to 68 or 70 for those who are presently under 50. People are living longer and healthier lives and can be more productive in their later years since technological advances mean that fewer activities require manual labor.

———

In the Athenian state in ancient Greece, people worked two days a year to pay taxes. Much has changed. When you have to work nearly half the year to pay taxes, you're basically working for the government. In that case, you don't have as much freedom to choose what you want to do with your life.

As the percentage of work going to the government increases (moving toward socialism), individuals have fewer choices, and more mandates from government. A truth throughout the history of civilization is that he who has the gold makes the rules. When the state has extorted the gold from the taxpayers, guess who makes the rules.

Likewise, if the government is the only source of jobs, you are forced to serve the whims of a monopoly.

I can't stress enough how important it is for people—especially upcoming generations—to understand that only through a system of private sector free enterprise can a country grow and prosper and fulfill growing aspirations.

There is a fundamental reason. Under freedom and free enterprise, you are free to keep most of what you earn or produce and make you own decisions about how you use it. Taking things away from people requires coercion or force. That requires big force or big government—and that's a slippery slope to authoritarianism, where most or all of your choices are taken away.

The best solution? Perhaps Johann Wolfgang von Goethe said it best: "What is the best government? That which teaches us to govern ourselves."[265] That is the antithesis of socialism.

---

265 http://quotes.liberty-tree.ca/quotes.nsf/ByName?SearchView. Accessed 11/2/15.

6

THERE IS NO THIRD WAY

Why Free Enterprise Capitalism Works Better Than Any Other System

"The philosophy of capitalism is the only moral system that
guarantees to man his individual liberty,
and therefore, the only valid political, economic,
and social standard for pursuing prosperity and peace."[266]

Matt Ridley

In the 1980s, two Romanian doctors, husband and wife, defected to the United States from communist Bucharest, Romania, by walking over the Carpathian Mountains and finding their way to Austria with nothing but the clothes on their backs.

They were brought to the U.S., where they were hosted by Catholic Charities and soon transferred to Washington D.C. They visited various neighborhoods, markets, shops, and restaurants, while their hosts extolled all that America had to offer. The Romanians, in turn, responded politely and thanked their hosts for showing them such beautiful locales.

Then they quietly asked to be taken to the places where they themselves could buy goods.

---

266 http://adamsmithslostlegacy.blogspot.com/2009/01/free-capitalist-13-january-here-carries.html. Accessed 6/28/17.

"Anywhere you want," they were told.

After a period of silent incredulity, they broke down in tears.

It was only when they realized the *freedom* of America that they finally understood the vastness of its possibility.

In Romania, no books on learning English had been allowed, as they were considered subversive. The couple had learned to speak English from Beatles records, and a smuggled book on teaching English—written in *French*. Needless to say, their accents needed a little work when they got to the U.S.!

Their first home in America was in Anaheim, California, just blocks from Disneyland. Every night, they sat on their back porch and tears came to their eyes when the fireworks went off; for the Romanian couple, they were a symbol of freedom.

They both went on to practice in the medical field in their new country and eventually became American citizens.

What Drives Progress

Progress is most prevalent where there is economic and personal liberty, and it lies at the heart of the experience of the two Romanian doctors who came to the U.S. What overwhelmed the couple was not so much the prosperity and resources of America, but the freedom to *participate* in that prosperity.

The greatest economic and personal liberties only exist where there are free people, free markets, and free enterprise. Those conditions, which form the basis for what we call capitalism, have inspired development of better, more cost effective products that enhance living standards throughout the world.

Socialists claim their goal is to help all their citizens, but as we have seen through numerous examples, such assertions are mostly theoretical. In real life, the principles of socialism don't work, and eventually lead to loss of freedom and, usually, to economic and societal collapse.

A free-market economy (capitalism) is an economic system where voluntary exchanges, (money, products or services), take place. The economic decisions made by individuals in such an arena are free-willed and de-centralized. The participants are able to act on their initiative without being ruled by a central authority. To be continuously and abundantly productive, people must be permitted to engage in work or projects of their choice, or, at the least, work that fulfills their hopes and capabilities. It is a key component of individual liberty.

How can you be free if you are ruled by a monopolistic, authoritarian government?

For freedom to endure, wealth and political power must be broadly based. This is sometimes called pluralism. Pluralism is an important part of a workable democracy and part of the foundation for assuring free enterprise and respect for property rights. It's a system in which everyone has a chance to better themselves.

In societies where people are allowed to own private businesses and accumulate wealth, the people are freer and more independent of government. They can make their own decisions—personal, vocational, and economic. Those individual decisions create increased individual productivity, and almost always then contribute to the productivity and well-being of society as a whole.

Contrast that with a society where decisions are centralized and made by government.

During his presidency, Barack Obama sometimes belittled business owners and said that people who created businesses "didn't do it by themselves. Other people did that." Presumably, he was primarily talking about infrastructure. Infrastructure has its place in the chain of productivity but government doesn't create productive businesses. It can only help create a favorable environment for them.

Government runs by taxation alone. It is the fundamental funding basis for government operations. Government bureaucracies (sometimes known as the deep state) are good at surviving. Like any organism, bureaucracies tend to grow and perpetuate themselves. That is why our founders attempted to create a system that would constrain government, its growth and its authoritarian tendencies. Since governments aren't good at creating businesses, they instead depend on successful ones to generate income, products, and services that can be taxed.

Prosperity comes to a country not through government, but through employment and the successful operation of small businesses and corporations—those created by entrepreneurial individuals who are willing to take risks to make new enterprises work and new jobs happen. Government is supposed to be kept to a minimum, its territory confined to those needs that can't be handled by the people themselves, such as defense, police and fire protection, and the building of infrastructure.

None of that happens unless there are taxes, and there are no taxes unless there are successful businesses and individuals to pay them.

The innovations that significantly raised the living standards of people began during the First Industrial Revolution. Manufacturing changed forever, and paved the way for the inventions that are familiar to us today. More recently, Bill Gates' Microsoft revolution, Steve Jobs' Apple revolution, and the Moore's Law revolution, would not have happened with the same dynamic results if left to socialist societies.

Why not? Because where the government owns the means of production, distribution, and exchange, there is less incentive for individuals to work hard and make things better. There is no profit. There is much less incentive to get things done promptly. The incentive is to cover one's posterior. What fabulous creations came out of communist Soviet Russia? Virtually none. Cuba? None. Venezuela? None.

And where did the iPhones come from? The electric cars? And the high paying jobs in the tech industry? They came from the entrepreneurial, free-market system where inventors created new products that serve the world, *and* reward both the innovators and the public at large.

A World Without Corporations

Walmart, Whole Foods, McDonald's, and other shopping havens throughout the world were not created by socialists. They are the products of the free market capitalist system and a corporate model.

What would our world look like without corporations?

The Soviet Union of the 1960s offers an answer: a drab landscape with virtually no progress, little business innovation, jammed public housing, and no way to move out of your rut of a job or space.

In a word, no *choice*. In the Soviet Union of the 1960s, there were very few private automobiles and limited consumer products. But there was an abundance of government regulation and control. And, there was the "Gulag" for non-conformers.

It is the large and small corporations and partnerships throughout the world that give us the vast selection of goods and services that we use every day. Do you want a cell phone, a washing machine, a car, a computer? You can get them in most countries. Fortunately, they keep getting better and less expensive. That means they are more broadly affordable.

Freedom—both to aspire and to meet aspirations—drives our progress.

It is corporations in a free market that make and distribute the variety of products we see in the world marketplace. And many of those who buy the products are able to do so because they have earned money working at those same companies and others like them.

Yet, many liberal commentators portray corporations as evil giants taking advantage of the public and making unfair profit. These are incendiary words designed to create unrest in those who wish to further socialist agendas.

Sally Kohn, a liberal commentator formerly on Fox News and now on CNN, believes that the "barriers to opportunity" are the result of "economic inequality baked into our society by giant corporations that have crippled our government and our community..."[267]

As delusional as this statement is, at least in the article Ms. Kohn admits that the conservative commentators she worked with were very nice people (Sean Hannity, Bill O'Reilly, etc.), and not demons as usually

---

267 Sally Kohn. "What I learned as a liberal talking head on Fox News," Christian Science Monitor online, 4/15/14. https://www.csmonitor.com/Commentary/Common-Ground/2014/0415/What-I-learned-as-a-liberal-talking-head-on-Fox-News. Accessed 9/25/19.

portrayed by some biased reporters. Kohn continues, though, to parrot the liberal party line that corporations are the problem in our society.

Corporations and partnerships are formed so that groups of people can do what individuals cannot do by themselves. Almost all corporations start small. Someone has an idea for a new or better product or service, or a way to create something less expensively. And, it almost always takes money (the "capital" in capitalism) to launch a business. The inventor is often richer in imagination than cash, so he or she has to convince someone else the idea is a good enough one to finance.

The first round of financing frequently comes from friends and family—people who believe in the individual even if the idea seems strange or impractical. They have the freedom to form a partnership or a corporation. The advantage of a corporation is that it limits liability—it's one thing to want to help a friend, it's another to be exposed to liability that could end up costing the friend everything he has.

Only a fraction of corporations succeed. Many die because: (1) the idea wasn't really all that good; (2) the development of the idea wasn't handled well; (3) the right talent wasn't assembled to make it work; (4) competition was too severe; (5) the timing was bad; or (6) the enterprise simply ran out of money—or all of the above.

A few, however, succeed. Some become big, provide an abundance of jobs, and propel society to a new level of productivity and prosperity—think Singer, Edison, Maytag, Ford, Boeing, Walmart, Microsoft and Apple, to name a few. They create employment for people, who can then, in turn, prosper by taking advantage of the opportunities for advancement that larger corporations offer. Larger companies often last through several generations, thereby providing greater job security.

Corporations are part of free enterprise capitalism. Free enterprise tends to be self-correcting. People don't continue to deal with those who would take advantage of them, so long as there is an alternative—competition. If a better way of doing things or a better price comes along, it is adopted—either by existing companies or by new ones. This makes markets more flexible and efficient.

Historically, this system of fusing of ideas, talent, hard work, and capital has given us the highest standards of living for the broadest range of people anywhere. In America, our Constitution, Bill of Rights, and the stable system of checks and balances have allowed businesses and all the people they employ to prosper. Our operating system has also given us the least corrupt major government in the world. The U.S. system isn't perfect, but to paraphrase Winston Churchill, it is just better than all the others.

The U.S doesn't have a monopoly on this system; we gladly share it with anyone in the world who wants to create something or strive for a better life. All it requires are the key ingredients: capital, and free people. They create the intellectual property that makes for better, more capable, higher quality and less expensive products and services. Everyone benefits and the world can ride to new levels of prosperity—provided bureaucratic regulation doesn't strangle the initiative. For this to work, there must also be solid respect for free enterprise and a stable government that will assure property rights so people get to keep the benefits of their hard work.

The $1,500 Sandwich

Corporations and partnerships of all sizes invest in research and development. This results in new products and services. Thanks to the internet and the information and communications revolution, things can be produced economically in smaller lots and there is greater access to distribution and promotion for small businesses than ever before.

In a world without corporations, however, things look quite different.

It was recently reported that an enterprising individual decided to make a sandwich for himself from scratch. "He grew the vegetables, gathered salt from seawater, milked a cow, turned the milk into cheese, pickled a cucumber in a jar, ground his own flour from wheat to make the bread, collected his own honey, and personally killed a chicken for its meat."[268]

He then published the results of his experiment, noting that to make the sandwich and all the ingredients took six months and cost him $1,500.

268 "The $1,500 Sandwich." WSJ, Opinion/Notable and Quotable. 9/27/15. http://www.wsj.com/articles/notable-quotable-the-1-500-sandwich-1443385713?mg=id-wsj; "How to Make a $1,500 sandwich in only 6 months." http://theawesomer.com/the-1500-6-month-sandwich/336854/. Accessed 10/9/15.

Think of what life was like when people grew all their food and made their own clothes, independent for the most part from corporations and trade. They were poor and their work was never done. Farmers still work long hours, but now they have the benefit of farm machinery, better farming techniques and higher producing crops, thanks to free enterprise and its incentives.

The risk-reward ratio is what drives decision-making for business. If there is a good potential reward waiting for you out there, you are more inclined to take the risk. Austrian economist Friedrich Hayek summarizes: "The construction of a new plant [or product, etc.] will only be justified if it is expected that the prices at which the product can be sold will remain sufficiently above marginal costs to provide not only amortization of the capital sunk in it but also to compensate for the risk of creating it."[269]

269 Friedrich Hayek. *Law, Legislation, and Liberty*: Vol. III, *The Political Order of a Free People*. Chicago: University of Chicago Press, 1981. At 130.

In other words, why do it if it's not profitable?

That's the beauty of our flexible free enterprise system: Those who want to take risks have the opportunity to do so, and the free market system will reward them if they are successful.

Risk-taking is an essential driver of progress and higher living standards. Entrepreneurial individuals tend to be more willing to take risks to accomplish their dreams. As Will Rogers said, "Why not go out on a limb? That's where the fruit is."

That logic doesn't apply in socialist systems.

Those who don't want to take risks can work for government, sometimes accept lower pay and have more security. The other side of that coin, though, is the lack of incentive to grow creatively.

> "Entrepreneurial business favors the open mind.
> It favors people whose optimism drives them
> to prepare for many possible futures,
> pretty much purely for the joy of doing so."
>
> Sir Richard Branson

Competition as the Great Stimulator of Progress

The free-enterprise corporate model operates at the other end of the spectrum from the socialist model where one "organization" (the government) controls the most significant enterprises. Unfortunately, that model strips away one of the great drivers of free-market economic systems: competition.

Progress evolves when people search for a better way. Competition encourages this. There's a reason that few great inventions come from the public sector: rewards for excellence are few. Surviving, rather than thriving, becomes the focus. Protecting one's backside becomes the end goal.

And what of the extraordinary profits, so often the focus of protests and criticism?

The Rev. Robert Sirico comments, "Even extraordinary profit margins serve a necessary function. High profits signal to other entrepreneurs that the public is demanding more of a particular good or service than is being produced."[270] This encourages new businesses and entrepreneurs to enter the field, which results in more products and competitive prices.

Larry Reed, of the Foundation for Economic Education (www.fee.org), says, "Profit is a measure of success." Profit is "fertilizer that quickens the imagination" of those who would produce.[271] Hayek points out what should be obvious to all, but is ignored by statists: Out of profit, "the successful obtain the capital for further improvements."[272]

Some movie stars, entertainers and star athletes have high earnings and become very wealthy. Perhaps some of them feel guilty about their wealth, and that is why many of them support socialist ideas. But while they earn millions, they complain that CEOs make much more money than the average worker. The media thrives on this and tends to reinforce their arguments.

Good CEOs, however, are like good quarterbacks—they take you to the Superbowl. That level of performance is worth a lot to teams, owners and communities.

By contrast, there is really no such thing as a "good" socialist quarterback, as socialist policies attempt to equalize everything, only to end up in mediocrity, and then failure.

In a socialist government, only the elites fare well. In a free-enterprise market, rewards are based on whatever the market will bear. A CEO won't keep his job if he doesn't sustain productivity and keep the profit margin up; a quarterback won't keep his job if he doesn't move the ball down the field and win games; an actor, director, or producer who fails to gain market share for his or her films will see earnings decline.

The same principle applies to all these situations, yet only corporate CEOs are vilified. The fact that a CEO makes a high salary does not mean that the average worker makes less. In fact, the opposite is usually

---

270 *Defending the Free Market*, Wash. D.C.: Regnery Publishing, 2012, at 88.

271 *Stossel*. Fox Business Channel. 2/16/16.

272 Friedrich Hayek. *Law, Legislation, and Liberty*: Vol. III, *The Political Order of a Free People*. Chicago: University of Chicago Press, 1981. At 130.

true. If the company does well, employees do well. If the company doesn't do well, employment and wages can drop or the jobs can go away, and the CEO can be fired.

At the beginning of the 20th century, the great innovators amassed incredible fortunes for themselves and their families. They were often called "robber barons," accused of making money at the expense of others. But they were innovators—they dramatically improved efficiency, produced innovations in many arenas, and lowered the price of steel, oil, and transportation.[273] In turn, they built the foundations for a strong and prosperous nation.

"The robber baron epithet is a ruse to raise hostility against economic freedom in favor of government overreach."[274] Matt Ridley calls the great innovators "enricher-barons."[275] By lowering the price of products and services, all Americans were enriched.

Great visionaries such as Cornelius Vanderbilt and James J. Hill rejected government subsidies and programs and built wealth through their innovations, and with invested funds—their own funds and those of investors. Their accomplishments were a great boon to all Americans who were able to take advantage of increasingly modern technology.

As Ayn Rand wrote, "America's abundance was not created by public sacrifices to the common good, but by the productive genius of free men who pursued their own personal interests and the making of their own private fortunes."[276]

John D. Rockefeller, who was called a robber baron himself, called the federal government the biggest robber baron of all. With constant, ever-increasing taxes, fees and assessments (most of which are very poorly utilized), the government takes away money that could be used much

---

273   Ed Farr. "The Robber Baron vs. The Government." RantLifestyle. 7/13/14. http://www.intel-lectualtakeout.org/library/business-and-economics/myth-robber-barons. Accessed 9/2/15.

274   http://www.rantlifestyle.com/2014/07/13/the-robber-baron-vs-the-government/. Accessed 9/2/15.

275   *The Rational Optimist* (2011). UK: Harper Collins. At 23.

276   https://www.quotes.net/quote/6413. Accessed 9/21/19.

more efficiently in the private sector to generate higher pay and higher living standards for everyone.

Milton Friedman believed the main reason for the greater efficiency of the private sector was that "the incentive of profit is stronger than the incentive of public service."[277]

The private sector constantly strives for innovation and progress, and makes room for anyone with better ideas and a strong work ethic.

"Creative Destruction"

Of course, when new products and services come to the market, it is inevitable that other products—even if well-established—will decline or fade away. Joseph Schumpeter, an Austrian-American economist and political scientist, called such an event "creative destruction."

Some may see this as one of the adverse effects of capitalism. But new products make new jobs, even if the old ones die away. You can see the effects of competition and creative destruction in the marketplace by looking at the history of some popular products.

Take the iPhone, for example. Blackberry dominated the market initially, but because the iPhone had new and more desirable features, and improved human efficiency, it changed the marketplace and replaced the Blackberry in a very short time. Most consumers would be reluctant to switch back.

The market lets you choose what you want from a variety of products; the best will usually win. That is the way progress happens: by improving on what's already available, and creating what isn't.

Improvement is what free enterprise stimulates and what government tends to slow down. If government had regulated cell phones and dictated, "All cell phones must have the features of the Blackberry," the iPhone would not have been developed.

Competition sometimes gets a bad rap, but without competition, there is less progress. Furthermore, we are now in a world economy where

---

277 Why Government is the Problem, at 8. Hoover Institution Press, 1st edition. February 1, 1993.

competition is not a choice. "Even if you're on the right track," Will Rogers once quipped, "you'll get run over if you just sit there."

Of course, you have to be careful not to take too much risk. If you're competing with the big guys, you had better be sure you have a real advantage that can be a balance against the strength they have built up through substantial market share. "Nourish your hopes but do not overlook realities," as Winston Churchill put it.[278]

When we first developed the Predator RPA (Remotely Piloted Airplane, a.k.a. drone) at General Atomics, we knew we had something new and revolutionary and, that it could cut defense costs dramatically. If we had tried to produce an improved F-16 fighter jet, we would have failed because we would have had nothing to offer that was significantly different, and we would have been unable to compete with the well-established aircraft companies.

But with the Predator, we had created an RPA that had unprecedented endurance, was reliable, and was relatively inexpensive. It had strong potential for persistent ISR (intelligence, surveillance and reconnaissance) and precision attack. Because of that, it significantly reduced loss of life for non-combatants. Predators have a decisive effect on the battlefield, saving the lives of soldiers while keeping pilots out of harm's way.

We estimate that during the height of the war in Iraq, for every 200 hours a Predator was in the air, one U.S. combatant's life was saved. That equates to about 1,000 lives in one year alone.

Equally important, thousands of civilian lives have been saved because of vastly improved and extensive ISR, and the precision of the Predator's "striker" weapons.

The result is that we have gained major market share in the serious RPA field. We must constantly innovate to keep it. We spend hundreds of millions of dollars on continual improvements. If we don't, someone will come along with something better and shove us out of the market.

---

278 www.azquotes.com/quote/848519. Accessed 8/19/15.

Friedrich Hayek puts it this way: "The very complexity of modern conditions makes competition the only method by which a coordination of affairs can be adequately achieved."[279]

Consider the opposite side of the creative destruction coin. In 1975, Kodak had a digital camera. Because they thought it would cut into their film sales, they declined to develop it. Now digital has mostly replaced film and Kodak has very little camera market share. They fell victim to what some call "the dark side of innovation"—they didn't see the future coming. Kodak, the great corporate institution, went bankrupt in 2012.[280]

Other companies have likewise resisted creative destruction and paid the price. Sony invented the transistor radio, the Walkman, and the Trinitron cathode ray tube and had a commanding share of that market. They didn't want to develop flat panel displays because doing so would have cut into the Trinitron market. They didn't develop flat panels, but others did. Now, Sony is no longer number one in consumer electronics.

Creative destruction is hard on companies that are inefficient. Private business organizations should be as "flat" as possible to be effective, thus eliminating layers of potentially redundant supervision, and reducing cost and time.

At General Atomics, we have very capable middle managers. We try to keep them to a minimum to keep overheads down. Because of that, we are generally able to move faster and with less expense than the competition. Our customers share in the benefits.

We, and other innovative companies, now have computer-aided design and manufacturing capability that shortens time and reduces costs of doing new things. In many cases, a design solution that can deliver 90% of the value of a new product can be delivered at only 10% of the cost of what the 100% solution would require.

---

279   The Road to Serfdom (condensed version), San Bernardino CA (2014).

280   They have since restructured and maintain headquarters in Rochester, NY, producing products in printing and packaging, software and film, and are currently developing photographer-oriented cryptocurrency.

I call this the "Goldin Rule"—named in honor of Dan Goldin, who headed NASA for ten years under three U.S. Presidents. Dan probably has more experience running high cost, high-risk technical projects than any other person in history. The Goldin Rule phenomenon is something he saw throughout his ten years in government and before that as a scientist, engineer, and executive with aerospace companies. He is also one of my surfing buddies.

One-hundred-percent solutions are expensive. The current F-35[281] development is a good example of the cost overruns[282] that happen when one airplane attempts to provide the 100% solution for the Air Force, Navy, and Marines—all in one basic airframe.

The history of airplanes that are adapted for all services is that they usually have to make too many compromises to fit too many diverse missions. Operating from a carrier, as the Navy does, adds weight and refinements that the Air Force doesn't need. Being able to take off and land vertically, which is what the Marines want, adds additional complications, weight, and cost. The result in each case is an airplane that costs too much and is suboptimal for each of the services.

All too frequently, government requirements and management overheads get in the way. The justification is that time and deliberation make for better products, but the evidence doesn't necessarily support the claim. Consider the development of the P-51 during WWII: while it now takes around twenty years for the U.S. government to come up with a new fighter jet, it took only six months to develop the P-51, which was arguably the best fighter in World War II.

The innovative cycle of creation and destruction drives progress and prosperity in free enterprise. In socialist societies the drive to innovate is not nearly as strong.

---

281 This Wikipedia article describes in detail the many cost overruns and delays in producing the F-35 fighter. https://en.wikipedia.org/wiki/Lockheed_Martin_F-35_Lightning_II#Program_cost_increases_and_delays. Accessed 9/2/15.

282 "Trump tweets that the F-35's cost is out of control…" http://www.businessinsider.com/lockheed-martin-stock-down-trump-tweets-f-35-costs-out-of-control-2016-12. Accessed 9/25/16.

Which Road: Serfdom or Prosperity?

The public policy roads that countries choose significantly impact the well-being of their citizens. Making choices is difficult and fraught with problems.

My first notions of the workings of the capitalistic system and the value of hard work came when I was about eight years old. One day in Denver, I watched men digging ditches with shovels and knew I didn't want to do that type of work all my life. I told my mother that I didn't want to be a ditch digger, and she responded that if I worked hard at school I would not have to. With education, she told me, I could do whatever I wanted.

That may be the reason that I have concentrated my efforts in life on innovation. Were it not for a free enterprise capitalist system, my life would probably have seen more frustration than accomplishment.

Of course, there is much disagreement over what road to take. Not everyone agrees that a free enterprise capitalist system is the right path. Some say capitalism favors only the rich. Yet, poor people don't get poorer because rich people get richer. "There are some arguments so illogical," says economist Walter Williams, "that only an intellectual or politician can believe them. One of those arguments is: capitalism benefits the rich more than it benefits the common man."[283]

The truth is far more inspiring: "What has made poor people richer? The same phenomenon that has made rich people richer: Capitalism."[284]

Pope Francis made strong statements against capitalism when he visited the United States in 2015, stating that the opposite of capitalism is cooperation. [285] In that, he is wrong. The opposite of capitalism is collusion, monopoly and, frequently, corruption. The very things that critics point to in condemning capitalism are, in fact, its antithesis.

---

283   Walter E. Williams , *Capitalism and the Common Man*, August 25, 1997. http://econfaculty.gmu.edu/wew/articles/97/cap-comm.htm. Accessed 10/21/15.

284   Daniel Hannan. www.capx.com/if-you-are-reading-this-youre-in-the-top-1-probably. 12/1/14. Accessed 7/15/2015.

285   William McGurn. "Pope Francis, Unfettered." WSJ: Opinion, Main Street. 9/22/15. http://www.wsj.com/articles/pope-francis-unfettered-1442875692?mg=id-wsj. Accessed 9/24/15.

It is unfortunate that the Pope got his impression of capitalism from the semi-socialist systems of Argentina and Brazil. He doesn't seem to understand that economic freedom leads to all the other freedoms and the most prevalent human rights.[286]

As George Gilder put it: "Under capitalism, a business prospers only if customers voluntarily trade for its output….Capitalism at its essence is a competition of giving. …The genius of Capitalism (and only Capitalism) is that it channels self-interest into altruism….Entrepreneurs can only help themselves by helping others."[287]

Brazil's former president, Dilma Rousseff, is a lifelong socialist/ Marxist. Her regime produced a disastrous economy, falling currency rates, a weak job market, and rampant corruption.[288] Brazilians impeached and removed her.

Yet fantasies of a socialist utopia continue.

In 2011, the well-known movie director Steven Spielberg said that he thought President Obama should declare a "temporary" dictatorship. Spielberg may have felt that was a good thing because at the time he agreed with the policies being implemented. The problem is that by definition a dictator eventually ends up doing what *he* wants, giving short shrift to the wishes of his subjects. With a dictatorship, there is no oversight: Congress and the courts would become irrelevant—the very opposite to the checks and balances system implemented by our wise Founders.

Similarly, the left-wing Rolling Stone magazine released a cover in 2014 with a headline advocating that America embrace full-blown communism.[289]

---

286 Paul Kiernan. "Brazil Output Shrinks More than Expected." WSJ, World News. 8/29-30/15. At A6.

287 George Gilder. "Why Capitalism Works." http://prageruniversity.com/Economics/Why-Capitalism-Works.html#.VcTUZPliqfM. Accessed 7/28/15.

288 Mimi Whitefield. "Brazil: How Could So Much Go So Wrong?" The Miami Herald. 11/1/15. http://www.miamiherald.com/news/nation-world/world/americas/article42134757.html. Accessed 11/8/15.

289 January 2014 issue. "Our New Year's wish," they intone.

The magazine apparently does not grasp the connection between the funding of social programs, and the programs themselves. In 2014, they advocated for a fully communist state, in particular because they believed it would help the millennial generation. They wanted a government-sponsored monthly stipend for all citizens, whether or not they work, because both unemployment and jobs "blow." They call it a "jaw-droppingly simple idea."[290]

They demanded:

- Guaranteed work for everybody
- Social security for all
- Take back the land from private ownership
- Make everything owned by everybody
- Put a public bank in every state [291]

The "jaw-droppingly simple solution" doesn't stand up to even modest scrutiny. Where do they think governments get their money? The answer is: *from people who work at jobs provided by corporations, small business, and sole proprietorships.* When those jobs disappear, so do the taxes to support welfare programs.

The article would be laughable if it weren't so pathetic. This outlook is typical of those who know nothing about economics or the sources of revenues. Why do they believe that a system that has created economic disasters like Venezuela would work here? Does Rolling Stone really advocate that owners and employers keep on working and paying into the system so that the funds can be distributed to all those who don't want to work? How long would that last?

---

290   Matthew Burke, "Rolling Stone Magazine calls for full-blown communism in America," 1/5/2014; http://www.tpnn.com/2014/01/05/rolling-stone-magazine-calls-for-full-blown-communism-in-america. Accessed 10/21/15.

291   "Rolling Stone Magazine Calls for Full Blown Communism in America." 1/5/14. http://www.tpnn.com/2014/01/05/rolling-stone-magazine-calls-for-full-blown-communism-in-america/. Accessed 10/21/15.

To those who study history and the vicissitudes of political states, such views are shocking. They demonstrate how left-wing politicians have succeeded in convincing nearly half the country that socialism would be a good thing for America. Despite high employment, low economic growth, and a weak foreign policy, half the electorate voted a second term for Barack Obama in 2012. The other half (and part of the first half) took a different approach in November 2016 when they voted for a free enterprise entrepreneur and businessman, Donald Trump..

World-renowned economist Milton Friedman would likely have approved. Phil Donahue, a popular talk show host years ago, asked Friedman whether he had doubts about capitalism. In his reply, Friedman summed up free enterprise brilliantly:

> "The great achievements of civilization have not come from government bureaus. Einstein did not construct his theory under orders from a bureaucrat. Henry Ford did not revolutionize the auto industry that way. In the only cases in which the masses have escaped from … grinding poverty…, the only cases in recorded history, is where they have had capitalism and largely free trade. If you want to know where the masses are worse off, it's exactly in the kinds of societies that depart from that. …[T]he record of history is absolutely crystal clear that there is no alternative way so far discovered of improving the lot of the ordinary people that can hold a candle to the productive activities that are released by the free enterprise system."[292]

There have been times in history when some people amassed wealth by pillaging their neighbors. Conquest was a fast way to get wealth, power and influence—if you needed something, you seized it. That's what most conquerors did throughout history. The human instinct to protect

---

292 http://www.brainyquote.com/quotes/quotes/m/miltonfrie412621.html.

family, property and country is very strong. In the popular 1995 movie, *Braveheart*, Mel Gibson (playing the historic Scotsman, William Walker), fought to the death to protect his rights against those who would take what he had.

A court of law is better than fighting to resolve disputes.

Walter E. Williams has observed that, rather than increasing wealth through looting, plundering and enslaving one's neighbors, "Capitalism made it possible to become wealthy by serving your fellow man."[293]

Critics say that capitalism is selfish—that it is people only thinking of themselves. But it's quite the opposite. The entrepreneur must determine what the public wants, and be able to provide it. The measure of entrepreneur's success is how well they have pleased their buyers—the public. Yes, successful entrepreneurs make profits, and so they should, but the aim of those products or services must be to serve others with better products if they expect to stay in business.

As Ayn Rand said,

> "Do not make the mistake of the ignorant,
> Who think that an individualist is someone who says
> 'I'll do as I please at everyone else's expense.
> An individualist is a man who recognizes the inalienable rights of man—
> His own and those of others."
>
> — Ayn Rand [294]

The capitalist system says, "I have a really good idea, I've done my due diligence, and I think my idea has value. I'm willing to put my heart and soul into it but I don't have the money to get the business going. If you would lend or invest, you put up the money, I'll put in the brains and the work, and we'll split 50/50."

---

293 http://econfaculty.gmu.edu/wew/articles.html; Aug. 25, 1997. Accessed 9/22/14.

294 http://www.galtsgulchonline.com/posts/a7ec4e/do-not-make-the-mistake-of-the-ignorant. Accessed 8/7/15.

That's what our system allows. We have angel capitalists, venture capitalists, private equity and public offerings. All of these contribute to, or are part of, providing the capital that makes it possible to develop projects and better products.

John Mackey, co-CEO of Whole Foods, concurs:

"The inventions that have changed the world—automobiles, telephones, gasoline, the Internet, antibiotics, computers, airplanes—didn't happen automatically or by government edict; they all required massive amounts of innovation. Human creativity, partly individual but mostly collaborative and cumulative, is at the root of all economic progress."[295]

Free people are simply more imaginative and productive.

When Donald Trump was elected President of the United States, liberal heads exploded. There were numerous protests in the streets (predominantly in California and New York), bemoaning his presidency, predicting a global meltdown because of his policies.

And what happened?

Through his entrepreneurial and free-market vision, the changes he made produced the lowest Black, Hispanic, Asian-American, and female unemployment in history. More Americans are now employed than ever before. New unemployment claims hit a 49-year low. Youth unemployment hit the lowest rate in nearly 50 years. Almost 3.9 million people have been lifted off food stamps. After tax cuts, $300 billion flowed back into the U.S. Small businesses. They now have the lowest top marginal tax rate in 80 years.

U.S. GDP grew about 50% faster than under Obama, who had said higher growth rates were no longer possible. Manufacturing jobs poured back into the U.S. Contrast that to Barack Obama's taunt that Trump would have needed a "magic wand" to bring back manufacturing jobs.[296]

---

295 *Conscious Capitalism: Liberating the heroic spirit of business.* Boston: Harvard Business Review Press, 2014.

296 https://thehill.com/blogs/blog-briefing-room/news/281936-obama-to-trump-what-magic-wand-do-you-have. Accessed 8/15/19.

The "magic wand"? Free market capitalism. Leftists don't seem to understand how free market capitalist economies operate.

The essence of a constitutional democracy is that freedom encourages free thought, and innovators and creators benefit from their work. The exceptional social gains made possible by this philosophy can be seen all over the world. China allowed private enterprise in 1978, and its society has transformed dramatically. Now, the Chinese need to show greater respect for other's property rights—intellectual and otherwise.

India is gaining in prosperity due to technological acceleration and a burgeoning private sector less burdened by government. Even parts of Africa are seeing rapid development.

None of this would have happened without the growing effect of free-enterprise and free-market capitalism. In some socialist countries previously plagued by rampant poverty, the populace is finally experiencing increasing prosperity thanks to capitalist ventures.

Supporters of socialism, conversely, tend to look to the short term and don't notice they are on the road to serfdom. Karl Marx didn't understand the potential for unlimited productivity, and the importance of growing economies. He focused on dividing the meager wealth that existed, rather than growing it. As one commentator noted, "Marx just didn't get it."[297]

Friedrich Hayek explains: "Capitalism creates the potential for employment. It created the conditions wherein people who have not been endowed by their parents with the tools and land needed to maintain themselves and their offspring..."[298] could be helped by others. Those "others" are the thousands of small business owners and the corporations, so vilified by the left, which provide millions of jobs in America and around the world.

Even Russia, the Putin totalitarian kleptocracy version of enterprise, has improved living standards over the old socialist totalitarianism called

---

297   David L. Prychito. Marxism." *The Concise Encyclopedia of Economics.* Indianapolis, IN: Liberty Fund, 2008. At 340.

298   F.A. Hayek, *The Fatal Conceit.* Chicago: University of Chicago Press, 1991. At 123.

Communism. Think of what they could do if the kleptocrats would get out of the way and Russians could have a real free enterprise system. . . . and success was less likely to land them in jail, or dead.

In a story from her law school days, a friend described how one of her professors, a Nigerian who had completed his undergrad at Oxford, spent his required year as an exchange student in Moscow in the 1960s. He kept up his Russian and his contacts and, as luck would have it, when communist Russia collapsed in 1991, this professor became the world expert on the Russian parliament, system of government, the new Russian business world, and Russian law.

He was hired by McDonald's[299] to open the first location in Moscow. He found that because the bureaucrats had lived their entire lives under communism, they had no idea how a capitalist enterprise operated. When he applied for a location, he was given an obscure space high up in an office building. He told them: "You have to understand that when you have a Big Mac[300] attack, you have to be on the ground floor."

Once that issue was settled and a ground floor space was secured, he had to negotiate with other countries to obtain the ingredients for making the hamburgers; Russia's communist society—unproductive and without entrepreneurial instincts—simply didn't produce what they needed.

The first Moscow McDonald's is the most frequented in the world, with lines around the block. It is considered so prestigious to work there that employees wear their uniforms around the clock, and the young employees earn more than their parents. The original Moscow McDonald's was open 24 hours a day from the start, and offered catering and private party rooms.

McDonald's is considered such an iconic American success that Russian President Vladimir Putin forced the closure of several locations in 2014 in retaliation for America's attempts to avert the Russian

---

299 The world's biggest hamburger fast food restaurant, available in 119 countries.

300 A double decker cheeseburger, one of the signature products of McDonald's. Having a "Big Mac attack" was pop lingo in the 1990s for wanting a Big Mac ASAP.

takeover of Ukraine.[301] He also forced merchants to remove Western goods from store shelves in August 2015, saying it was because they were contaminated, though it seemed clear that it was in response to sanctions against Russia.[302]

An enterprise like McDonald's could never have existed before capitalist projects were allowed in Russia. Once limited, free-enterprise captured the imagination of the Russian people, their lives improved dramatically—even though Putin, the authoritarian, has had trouble leaving it alone.

Why Doesn't Free Enterprise Do Well in Popularity Polls?

It's no exaggeration to say that free enterprise has transformed the planet. The competitive business landscape is responsible for almost all the innovation we take for granted, and the free market has lifted much of the world from abject poverty.

So why does it get such a bad rap?

Walter Williams laments that capitalism doesn't do well in popularity polls because "capitalism is always evaluated against the non-existent utopias of socialism or communism."[303]

It is much easier to articulate a message that "people are poor; we should do something about it," rather than a conservative message requiring at least some knowledge of how economics works.

Frank Luntz, a political commentator, pollster, and "public opinion guru" says that if Americans don't believe in economic freedom and our exceptional economic system, we are lost as a country. "One hundred years from now, historians will look back and say it's because Americans turned to socialism that America lost its way."[304]

---

301 http://www.newsmax.com/Newsfront/russia-closes-mcdonalds/2014/08/20/id/589898/. Accessed 8/22/14.

302 Paul Sonne and Ellen Emmerentze Jervell. "Russia Pulls More Western Goods Off Store Shelves." WSJ, World News. 8/26/15. At A7.

303 http://econfaculty.gmu.edu/wew/articles/97/cap-comm.htm. Accessed 10/20/15.

304 *Stossel*. 2/16/16. Fox Business Channel.

For an example, we need only to look to Great Britain, which turned to socialism soon after WWII, to see the economic consequences. The late Margaret Thatcher and other leaders have struggled to get back to free enterprise.

The "have nots" resent the luxuries that rich people have. But remember that everything considered a luxury is made or provided by people who get paid for what they do—whether that means making fancy cars, fancy homes or fancy foods. Providing those products and services means jobs.

Most poverty and undernourishment is caused by bad political systems. Drought and other acts of nature happen, but productive and well-organized societies can provide for necessities even under extreme conditions, so long as there is political stability. Where there is no political stability, we see famines, as in Africa today where warring factions frequently use food as a weapon by inhibiting its distribution.

Jeffrey T. Brown, of The American Thinker, believes those on the liberal left have "wholly abandoned such concepts as freedom, liberty, loyalty, and honesty." They know it's easier to steal than to earn a living, and if they can't justly receive what they need, they'll gladly take it by force. "Those practicing these trades as politicians, celebrities, officials, judges, and even citizens have cynically rejected the social code that enabled their own success, and have replaced it with the tyranny that will enrich them at the expense of other Americans."[305]

"Liberals often denounce free markets as immoral," notes Williams. "The reality is exactly the opposite. Free markets, characterized by peaceable, voluntary exchange, with respect for property rights and the rule of law, are more moral than any other system of resource allocation."[306]

---

305 Jefferey T. Brown, *Which will we choose: Our America or Theirs?* American Thinker, Nov. 1, 2014. http://americanthinker.com/articles/2014/11/which_will_we_choose_our_america.html. Accessed 2/17/16.

306 Walter Williams. *Compassion Versus Reality.* Townhall magazine, June 6, 2007. http://townhall.com/columnists/walterewilliams/2007/06/06/compassion_versus_reality/page/full. Accessed 11/4/14.

"[F]or the ordinary person, capitalism, with all of its warts, is superior to any system yet devised to deal with our everyday needs and desires."[307]

Capital markets (think stock market), venture capitalists, private equity funds, banks and other entities make capital available to people who are founding and running businesses that provide jobs. The system is structured so that if the deal isn't good for both sides, it doesn't happen—the participants look around for a better deal. Where there are free markets, monopolies can't last. There are alternatives. There are people around to innovate and compete. Capital markets make competitive ideas happen. It's due to the great ability to match money to ideas that we in America have had continuing and dramatic economic growth—greater than any other place in the world.

And to those who say that financial markets are only for the rich and don't apply to them, you might ask: Do you have a company or government retirement plan? If your answer is yes, you're in the stock market. If you own real estate, or pieces of private ventures, you will likely enjoy the benefits of free markets.

David Mamet observes that: "The Free Market is not a fantasy. We see its efficiency when the power goes out, when we are stranded in an airport, when we throng to the new exciting business down the block— the desire to exchange goods and services in order to increase individual happiness also increases *group* and *societal* happiness. The curtailment of that freedom leads to shortages, famine, and oppression."[308]

Is American youth's most recent infatuation with socialism reversible? Maybe, but it won't be easy. We need to get the message out that socialism just *isn't* the way to a world of high human productivity and freedom.

---

307 Walter Williams. "Capitalism and the Common Man." http://econfaculty.gmu.edu/wew/articles/97/cap-comm.htm. Accessed 8/17/15.

308 *The Secret Knowledge* (2012). NY: Sentinel (Penguin). At 93.

"A man who chooses between drinking a glass of milk
and a glass of a solution of potassium cyanide does not choose
between two beverages; he chooses between life and death.

A society that chooses between capitalism and socialism
does not choose between two social systems;
it chooses between social cooperation and the
disintegration of society.

Socialism is not an alternative to capitalism;
it is an alternative to any system
under which men can live as human beings."[309]

- Ludwig von Mises

Profile in Freedom: Gary Kasparov

Garry Kasparov is a Russian and world chess champion, and a pro-democracy activist. He is Chairman of the Human Rights Foundation in New York. Once ranked the #1 chess player in the world, Kasparov is now a tireless advocate for democracy and a symbol of resistance to the policies of Vladimir Putin.

He tried to run as a candidate in the 2008 Russian presidential process, but was unable to launch an effective campaign. He said that the political climate in Russia made it very difficult for opposition candidates to run. He is currently on the Board of Directors of the Human

---

309 Ludwig von Mises. *Human Action*, 676, 680. http://mises.org/quotes.aspx?action=subject&subject=Socialism. Accessed 10/7/14.

Rights Foundation in New York, and chairs its international division.

Kasparov took part in the Democratic Party of Russia, and later was instrumental in setting up "The Other Russia," in opposition to Putin. In 2007 he was briefly arrested following a demonstration, and a former KGB agent later said that Kasparov "was probably next on the list."

In 2012 he was beaten and arrested outside the court hearing the case of the rock band, Pussy Riot, but the charges were later dropped. In 2013 he wrote: "Fascism has come to Russia....Project Putin, just like the old Project Hitler, is but the fruit of a conspiracy by the ruling elite. Fascist rule was never the result of the free will of the people. It was always the fruit of a conspiracy by the ruling elites!"[310]

In 2014, Kasparov became a citizen of Croatia, having found it more and more difficult to live in Russia.

The Challenge: understanding and preserving freedom
"America is like a healthy body and its resistance is threefold: Its patriotism, its morality and its spiritual life.
If we can undermine these three areas, America will collapse from within.

- Joseph Stalin[311]

---

310   https://imrussia.org/en/analysis/politics/388-russia-a-test-on-fascism.
311   General Secretary of the Communist Party of the Soviet Union (1922-1953).

"In general, the art of government
consists in taking as much money as possible
from one party of the citizens to give to the other."[312]

- Voltaire[313]

What comes to mind when the average person thinks about "freedom?"

The ability to move about freely? The freedom to speak your mind? The opportunity to seek out whatever vocation or career appeals to you? The capability to earn a living and spend your money as you wish, buying the products and services you want to have, products that are created on an open market? The chance for your kids to do as well or better than you?

Can such goals be reached under socialism?

The answer is: no—it may sound good, but it doesn't work.

Look at free enterprise society and what you see are people who have the liberty to follow their dreams and strive toward their goals without being hampered by a dictatorial government.

Look at socialist societies and what you see is poverty, loss of liberty, and a minimal selection of goods and services.

The American economist Henry Hazlitt (1894-1993) said, "The whole gospel of Karl Marx can be summed up in a single sentence: Hate the man who is better off than you are. Never under any circumstances admit that his success may be due to his own efforts, to the productive contribution he has made to the whole community. Always attribute his success to the exploitation, the cheating, the more or less open robbery of others. Never under any circumstances admit that your own failure may be owing to your own weakness, or that the failure of anyone else may

---

312 "Money." (1770).

313 Nom de plume of Francois-Marie Arouet, French Enlightenment historian, philosopher, and writer.

be due to his own defects — his laziness, incompetence, improvidence, or stupidity." [314]

Today we are facing choices between serfdom and freedom. As Ludwig von Mises points out, there really isn't a third way: it's free enterprise capitalism, where everyone takes responsibility for themselves, or it's public sector authoritarianism. The latter squelches creativity and competition and leads to a dismal, dreary, non-productive society. Eventually, socialism, communism, tribalism, or totalitarianism lead to gross underachievement, declining living standards, loss of freedoms, and ultimately, collapse.

Should that be our "operating system" model?

There's no third way. Anything but the choice of freedom is a decision to start down the slippery slope that leads to privation and servitude.

"Freedom is never more than one generation away from extinction. We didn't pass it to our children in the bloodstream. It must be fought for, protected, and handed on for them to do the same.

— Ronald Reagan

"Democracy is the worst form of government except for all those other forms that have been tried from time to time."

Winston Churchill[315]

Should we choose the harsh truism identified by Voltaire and the cynicism of Stalin or the clear minded but realistic perspectives of Churchill and Reagan?

---

314 https://www.goodreads.com/quotes/670650-the-whole-gospel-of-karl-marx-can-be-summed-up. Accessed 9/21/19.

315 Winston Churchill, James C. Humes. *The Wit and Wisdom of Winston Churchill*. NY: HarperCollins, 1994, at 28.

7

CHOOSING FREEDOM

America at the Crossroads

"America will never be destroyed from the outside.
If we falter, and lose our freedoms,
it will be because we destroyed ourselves."
--Abraham Lincoln

Aldous Huxley's futuristic sci-fi classic, *A Brave New World*, details a sterile world where individualism has been more or less wiped out. It is a gloomy place, one where happiness mostly exists in "feelie" movies that stimulate the senses.

Writing during the political upheaval of the 1930s, Huxley was concerned the public might become subjugated by "the sophisticated use of mass media."[316] It seems a prophetic vision when we look at the power of the left-leaning media today.

Huxley's dark future stands in stark contrast to Kahn's Great Transition, the vision that opened this book. One is a future filled with promise and prosperity, a world where a rising tide lifts all boats. The other is a world where active freedom has been slowly but surely

---

316 http://clerkhouse.tumblr.com/post/80594427783/4-works-by-aldous-huxley-free-pdfs. Accessed 9/22/14.

transformed into passive acceptance of authoritarian systems that control the people in them.

As we reach the end of this book, the remaining question isn't which one of these futures is better. I hope that in these pages I've made the power of a free and enterprising society abundantly clear.

What we must turn our attention to now is the acknowledgment that both of these futures entail *choice*. As citizens in a free and democratic society, *we* get to choose the operating system on which our future is built. Each time we cast a vote, we're voting not only for an individual, but for the system and ideas that we believe are the right ones to carry us into the prosperous future that Kahn predicted.

The Power of Choice

Everyone makes choices, and the leaders of nations are no exception. Those choices are proven by time to be good or bad.

Kaiser Wilhelm of Germany made a bad choice in supporting Austria's revenge against Bosnia for one radical Serbian's assassination of Arch Duke Franz Ferdinand. The Kaiser's decision plunged the world into World War I and unbelievable carnage—after nearly 100 years of relative European peace.

Hitler made disastrous decisions for Germany at a time when Germans were chafing under the punitive terms of the Treaty of Versailles and vulnerable to a despotic psychopath. The carnage of WWII followed.

The Imperial Japanese made bad decisions that led to the bombing of Pearl Harbor. Lenin led Russia into socialism and communism. Mao did the same thing for China. Castro and his communist ideas ruined Cuba. More recently, Chavez and Maduro did the same for Venezuela. Kim Jong Un's communist authoritarian choices for North Korea stand in vivid contrast to South Korea, where per capita GDP (and living standard) is some 50 times greater.

Assad's desperate hold on power has decimated Syria, precipitated 500,000 deaths and the refugee crisis in Europe, and enhanced the disastrous ISIS and al Qaeda diversions. The totalitarian Khomeini regime of Iran is fomenting bloodshed and instability in the Middle East. Death, poverty, and stagnation is the result. These regimes shouldn't be allowed to survive in a civilized world.

Operating systems matter. *Choices* matter. And our decisions on who and what set of ideas will represent us best matters perhaps most of all.

Most destructive governmental decisions have a common theme: authoritarian, totalitarian leadership. It's a process that starts with control of the economy. Once authoritarian elites control the engines of the economy, freedoms are sharply reduced. Seizing other people's property and distributing it to supporters helps maintain control. And if economic control fails—as it so often does in authoritarian states—there is always imprisonment. Or execution, for those who would challenge it.

The alternative—the best one that we know of—is to follow the path of the choices made by our Founding Fathers. They were serious students of human behavior, of history, and of all forms of governance. They put the best lessons of humanity in our Declaration of Independence, the Constitution, and the Bill of Rights. They drew on their knowledge of history and human experience to set up a government with broadly shared and separated powers, pluralism, checks and balances, free enterprise, and protection of property rights. Our constitution-based operating system is largely self-correcting based on the simple principle that if an action is not broadly beneficial, it is rejected.

Our government wasn't, and isn't, perfect, but it is better than any other in history. Our operating systems, local, state, and national, do a relatively good job of balancing disparate interests and requirements—all while stimulating an economic engine that tends to lift people and enrich lives under conditions of maximum freedom.

The Road of No Return

The principal reason I have written this book is to convey the story of free enterprise as the operating system for prosperity and liberty for all. It is my hope that readers will understand the relationship between free enterprise and all other freedoms—and why socialism is a dead end.

The ideas expressed in this book do not originate with me. I build on the truths and wisdom of the ancient Greeks and Romans, the Magna Carta, Hayek, Friedman, Socrates, Alexander, Churchill, Reagan and many others including Mac Donald, Herman, Augustine, Will, and Hanson, in the hope that people will take away a message of freedom. That is what can change the world.

My urgency, however, stems not just from the trajectory of recent events, but from a compelling lesson from history that I believe is often overlooked: *when you lose freedom, it's very hard to get it back.* History shows that the slippery slope of socialism and the erosion of freedom are difficult to reverse; to undo them completely is a task of epic proportion, if it can be done at all. Sixty years of totalitarianism in Cuba is an example.

I am an optimist and believe in a bright future for humanity. But there is also the possibility that we could lose everything in our country, just as the Greeks and Romans did. We could lose our prosperity and way of life as oil rich Venezuela has done. It is possible our freedom and prosperity may ultimately represent only a footnote to the broad history of elitist authoritarianism that has predominated throughout most of history, over thousands of years.

Yes, our country has been going strong for almost a quarter of a millennium. Yet, if the leftward trajectory of recent years is allowed to continue, all bets are off. Radical leftists like Saul Alinsky and George Soros have stated their life's goal as the destruction of America as we know it. If history has taught us anything, it's that *it could happen.*

As Ronald Reagan once said, "Those who have known freedom and then lost it, have never known it again." We cannot protect our freedom enough. We cannot begin too soon. Stand up for free enterprise and let your voice be heard.

The Rising Tide of Freedom

When Thomas Hobbes described life in 1651 as "solitary, poor, nasty, brutish and short," serfdom was the norm, just as it had been through most of history. Life expectancy in Hobbes' time was about 30 years.

Income per person in his native England, which was far above most of the world, was about $5 a day, and that's in 2019 dollars.

Thanks to the Industrial Revolution and the Great Enrichment that followed, the typical Brit today lives to almost 80 and has an income of over $100 a day—a twenty fold improvement in productivity and well-being.

This is the power of choice, and the path of the future for everyone. This is the decision before us. We can choose a world of unlimited and environmentally sound energy resources. A world built on the opportunities of modern science, the communications revolution, artificial intelligence, and all the implications of Moore's law, and a world that knows freedom, peace, and prosperity. Rising tides really do lift all boats.

This is not a utopian pipedream. It *is* possible. But, it leaves out socialism.

It begins by making the right decisions. It begins with choosing a governance and operating system that increases everyone's productivity and well-being—a system where people get to keep most of what they work for.

Herman Kahn's great 400-year transition is upon us. It is lifting living standards and reducing poverty worldwide—and it can continue if we make the right choices. The rewards to civilization in peace and prosperity can be virtually unlimited. But if we listen to the siren songs of socialism and authoritarianism instead, the great transition won't happen. There could even be regression like we have seen in many parts of the Middle East and Venezuela.

In late September of 2001, Romanian writer, Cornel Nistorescu, penned a newspaper article entitled "Ode to America." In it, he mused on the solidarity of the American people following the World Trade Center disaster. He was struck by the magnanimity of strangers helping strangers, even at the risk of death, and of the successful people who enlisted and gave up their lives fighting in Iraq for what they believed in.

At the end of the article, he said he could come to only one conclusion: "Only freedom can work such miracles."[317]

Or as Daniel Hannan astutely opined: "The essence of America is freedom."[318]

That is not something that should be lightly discarded.

I believe everyone in the world can have the benefits of the productivity and well-being that the United States has developed. We already see major increases in productivity and reduction of poverty in many parts of the world. Everyone can have prosperity and freedom if they make the right choices.

Freedom works. With it, we can secure a prosperous, sustainable and remarkable future.

---

317   *Ode to America*. The Daily Event, Evenimentul Zilei, Bucharest, Romania. September 24, 2001. http://www.snopes.com/rumors/soapbox/nistorescu.asp. Accessed 11/1/14.

318   Daniel Hannan, *The New Road to Serfdom*. New York: Broadside Books/Harper Collins, 2010. At 2.

WITH GRATITUDE . . . .

This book was more work and more fun than I expected primarily because of the heavy lifting of research, recording of my thoughts and drafting, editing and compilation by Laura Dee. Laura was always cheerful, kept me focused on the project, and pushed me when necessary.

My wife Ronne, Rear Admiral US Navy retired, was a constant inspiration and foil for philosophical and practical ideas about how government really works. Son Austin, a strong historian and entrepreneur, gave me many insights that I was lacking. Daughter Virginia, a practicing psychologist, was a good reminder of the importance of economics and passing on important ideas to grandchildren. Dan Clements contributed to the organization and flow of the narrative.

Herman Kahn, who invited me to join the Hudson Institute board nearly forty years ago, intensified my interest in public policy and demonstrated how thinking about the future and being right on major issues, can make great difference in how events play out and history is made. Herman, Max Singer, Herb London, Ken Weinstein, General Bill Odom, Arthur Herman, John Walters, Scooter Libby, Walter Russell Mead and all the towers of wisdom at Hudson intensified my interest in challenging "Conventional Wisdom." Hoover Institution, with Victor Davis Hanson, Ayaan Hirsi Ali Ferguson, and Niall Ferguson are also inspiring. The USS Midway Museum, its creative CEO Mac McLaughlin and film producer Fleming Fuller are exercising new initiatives with video documentaries to teach the history of our Founders' ideas for freedom and how we as a nation have fought for those ideas.

My brother Neal has shown, through over sixty years of partnership, how big ideas can work—if you work hard enough at them even when exploring new and foreign fields. Our parents and grandparents gave support and stability and I am grateful every day. They were always willing to give us the benefit of the doubt that we could succeed, even when the risks were high—and a loose rein (freedom) that made success possible.

Neil Armstrong, Dan Goldin, Dr. Jim Lemke, Harry Combs, Larry Ashton, John Walton and many others showed me the power of science, engineering and innovation can make incredible things work on budgets that are within reach. Hugo Uyterhoeven, one of my professors at the Harvard Business School, dramatized the importance of business strategy—doing the right things at the right time.

And, greatest of all, Domingo Trueba and Ñongo Puig gave their lives for freedom, as my understanding of the value of Freedom went from abstractions, introduced in high school, studied at Yale, and taken for granted. These abstractions became the harsh reality of losing my freedom, completely, in Cuba.

APPENDIX

Linden's 1961 Letters to Domingo Trueba's Widow

In 1961, following my release from Fidel Castro's infamous prison in G2 headquarters in Havana, Cuba, I learned of the tragic execution of my cell mate and friend, Domingo Trueba. Domingo would likely have been one of the new leaders of a free Cuba if the military intervention had succeeded.

Upon learning the heartbreaking news of Domingo's death, I wrote two letters to his widow, Marta Trueba. It was my hope that furnishing her with details of Domingo's last days might bring her a little peace, or at least some closure.

After too much time, I have finally reconnected with Domingo's daughter Martica. She has provided me with copies of my original letters to her mother. At the time of the writing, there were no computers, only manual typewriters, and no spell check or auto correct. I appreciate the reader's indulgence of my errors, and present the letters here in their original form.

Pictures are from better times and letters follow. They are reprinted by permission of Martica Trueba.

Domingo Trueba and Cousin Carmina Trueba de Mestre

MARTA AND DOMINGO

DAUGHTER MARTICA AND DOMINGO

MANUEL ÑONGO PUIG AND WIFE OFELIA

HACIENDA TIERRA DORADA

G2 Headquarters Privat Residence
14 Street & 5 avenue
In Front of Residlet gred San Martin, Miramar

HERMANOS BLUE, HAMM, SMITH & CIA, LTDA

APARTADO 6 - MANAGUA, NICARAGUA - CABLE BLUBANOS

4 July, 1961

Dear Mrs Trueba,

   I have only now been able to bring myself to believe the fate of Domingo. I send you and your family my deepest heart rendering sympathy.

   Though I only knew Domingo for the 9 days we were in G2 headquarters together, March 24 to April 2 I came to revere him as a Prince and love him as a brother.

   His loss is a wound to me that will never heal. I will never draw an unlabored breath until the things he fought for become reality.

   I will keep in touch with you as the years pass in the hope that someday I might do something for you and your family.

   With most profound personal regards for Domingo and his family, sincerely,

15 October, 1961

Estimada Doña Martha,

I was most happy to recieve your letter of a couple of months ago.
So much that I had thought and wished to say about Domingo swelled
up and demanded immediate enunciation. I began to write you
immediately, but found it very difficult to capture the intensity
and depth and breadth of my feelings. There is so much to say
that I found myself beginning a chronicle that I hope someday will
take the form of a book . . . . that will partially explain the greatness
of Domingo and the terrors that are Cuba today.

For this moment, since I have long wanted to tell you of part of my
life with Domingo, and since my long chronicle will take a great deal
more time. . . . .a few of my most vivid memories of Domingo and
my days with him/

By 10:00 in the evening, about 11 hours after we had been forced to
land at Havana by a jet trainer converted to fighter, we were ordered
to our feet in the room we had returned to after interrogation. It had
been hot, stuffy, dark with the others who had been brought in that
day to B-2 headquarters. The hours of waiting, expectancy anxiety
hot smokey air breathing had numbed us to complacency on the piece
of butchers paper spread out on the marble floor. We rationalized
that in case we should get out immediately, we would want to be as
unfatigued as possible. We had been 60 percent sleep drousing when
the light came on again. It happened this way about every 15 minutes
I guess. The intervals could have been 5 minutes or hours. This
time instead of a few being picked over and taken out or some few ones
brought in, we were all told to get up. A few blue t' shirts were passed
out to some of the men. Swenson and I recieved none, perhaps the
maddness of this detention was about to end, maybe we were to be
released.

Instead, we were told to follow the rest of the group. If not to be released
at least perhaps they were taking us to jail cells were we could have a
cot and be released to real sleep. Out of the first processing room
into the hall way. A few scraggly bearded, cigar smoking, sub machine

gun holding, green clad slouchy young guards lounged in the halls. We eyed them with suspicion and they sneered back with little annimation, this was merely a procession ag of which they had seen many. To the end of the short hall, a stairway went up to the right, a plywood door was straight ahead, we turned left to face another plywood door which was unbolted and opened. The door opened on a black hold, yet the feeling that there was life inside came through the open door, they heat and stench as the air from what must be a room pushed its way past us . Except for the putrid odor, it was as if the door had been the door to a furnace or a steam room. Then the light flashed on. Eyes deap and tired stared out from drawn faces unshaven, blinked at the light. A murmor of resigned discontent passed as those approximately 35 inside beheld our group of eight which was to be deposited upon them-—much as a garbage collector deposits another can full on the truck.

The room had been completely full before we were pushed inside. Calculations laboriously made on subsequent days would indicate it was about 14' X 12. A few double deck Army bunks bunks lined the walls. One bunk saged particularly, a huge man propped himself half up to view the new arrivals. His black beard showed he had been there for several days. Lines in his face showed strength and maturity. His rough, angular, handsome face complemented his large and apparently powerful body. He spoke softly in a low, resonant, comanding voice in Spanish . . . . "there is always room for more, give them a place to lie down".

The light went out as abruptly as it had come on. I had saved my piece of butchers paper from the other room, spread it out on the floor once again, now several could sleep on it. It was a couple feet wide and six long. Swenson and I were the last in, we stayed at the doorway. The others lay down and we found that we to could lay down if I would wiggle half way beneath a bunk next to the door. I lay down partly under the bunk , Swenson lay down beside me. To turn over during the night; I had to move partly out from under the bunk, push Swenson over a little The night passed, the aches of the marble floor were subdued in drowse, then sleep.

Light of the morning creeped across the room. There was no reason for getting up, there was no reason to remain lying down. The urgency of sleep to tired body had been most earnesly satisfied, now the marble

- 2

foor dominated the senses, refused to allow further sleep. The
cieling was a dirty cream color, the walls a dirty brown, the bunk
above my nose, gray painted steel, the body on the bunk tan with
black hair, where the naked springs of the bunk pressed into his skin,
his skin in those places was pink and whitej

The room came to life slowly. More frequent the bodies turned over,
more frequently coughs, then a match scratched and somebody was
smoking. Somebody asked for a match and there were more wispers.
I sat up against the wall, Swenson did the same and had a cigarette,
somebody went to the water closet. The big man spoke.

"Vamos a organizar, vamos a organizar" attention flashed in everyone.
It was the same powerful, soft and compelling voice they had reacted
to in ahx half sleep in the night before. The big man lepped out of his
top bunk and stood in the middle of the others. . . some lying down,
some sitting proped against bunks and walls, some now standing.
He wore boxer undershorts, the rest was well conditioned, finely proportion
muscular mass.

He spoke in Spanish welcoming these who had come late last night to the
"Biblioteca", and laying the basic rules of the room for making living
as tollerable as possible------no smoking after the lights go out at night
because of the heat generated from 40 cigarettes or cigars in this xxxxx
small room, everyone take thxxdx their turn at cleanup detail twice per
day, no depositing ashes anywhere but in cups or cans, no spitting on
the floor, whenever water was running, fill the storage cans so we would
have water when it was not flowing. All the points obvious, but before
he had come, there had not even been this order. These basic steps
toward cleanliness and cooperation had made the little room a much
more kx wholesome place in which to pass 24hours per day for an
indefinite period. They called the big man "Cabo". This was Domingo
Trueba.

Swenson looked puzzled, Domingo picked it up immediately and gave
a rendition of his comments in English with an additional welcome to
us as foreigners in his country. His eyes keen and bright, his smile
broad and warm. Don and I felt better from this display of
friendship, we as north americans still had a strong friend in Cuba.

MCT   4   15 October, 1961

But this was not enough, Domingo quickly translated his welcome
back to Spanish so his country men could know what he had said
and with that there was general acclaim and approval of his welcome.

The Cabo had been introduced to this room, much in the same way
we had been some 4 days earlier. His beard and his bunk spoke for
his seniority. . . . . bunks were allocated as men left, usually it
took three days of the marble floor for there to be enough turn over
for a man to earn a bunk. For men who had come in at the same time
when there were fewer bunk vacancies than men, there was an ellaborately
ceremonial drawing of torn pieces of paper out of a box. Some of the
pieces had "cama" ix written on them, some did not.
        (bed)

Others had been there much longer than Domingo the "Capitan" had
been there for some 45 days. The Capitan had been in the mountains
fighting , first for Fidel but more recently against him. The Capitan
had been an excellent soldier, he had killed many men in Fidel's
militia. He was a sure candidate for the Paredon. Before going to
fight for Fidel, he had been a small farmer. That was long ago and
all lost now.

Inspite of his relatively few days, Domingo was transcendent. All men
accepted his authority. It had been this way from the day he came into
the room, from the moment he spoke.

Cafe con leche was served hot from a garbage pail, we ate white bread
with it, frequently soaking it in the coffee to make it more easily teath
torn. Domingo insisted that the honored foreign guests be served first,
and toasted our many happy returns to Cuba. After ourselves the
delicious (by comparison to what we had expected) liquid and bread
was passed around to the others. The Cabo made certain that that
this was done with maximum speed and efficiency. He ate and drank
when all others were provided for.

Breakfast over, the day could begin. There was business to be done.
The "Cooperativo de la Biblioteca" now disbursed the morning ration
of fruit juice that was instrumental in maintaining our health. The Cabo
explained in both English and Spanish that the cooperative had been
established in order that those who had no money, of whom he was one,
would still have available the necessities of fruit juice and cigarettes and

cigars that the guards would purchase for the inmates. The
Cooperativo would also strive to secur.e such as yet unavailable
luxuries as toilet paper, soap, tooth paste. Domingo explained
that all people in the room would benefit from the purchases of
the cooperative, regardless of ~~their~~ their ability to contribute.
We were unable to contribute anything, some were able to contribute
a few cents, others recieved ~~some~~ small ammounts of money from
relatives ~~who~~ who were lucky enough to locate them and visit them on ~~the~~
Sunday afternoon. ~~Theckweeeeeee~~

Domingo Trueba, treasurer of the Cooperativo de la Biblioteca
made the extatic report that the treasury of the Cooperative held
17 pesos that morning. This meant a reserve for approximately
three days. Nine days later the reserve capital of the Cooperativo
stood at 97 pesos. It seemed the Cabo was something of a good business
manager in addition to his other capacities.

Concerning security and ~~xxxx~~ discussions of what the different
individuals had or had not been doing as cause ~~xbxtx~~ for ~~thxrbx~~ their
interrment, Domingo wisely and frankly couseled that there were
doubtless spies in our ~~mxrbx~~ midst and that all should refrain from
discussions of that nature. This was as matter of fact as the 17 pesos
in our treasury but not to be worried about, just headed.

Domingo was gay and ebulent, more as though he were attending a
debutante ball. The men felt his spirit and there ~~was~~ were smiles
and generosity. Domingo came over to us, the business of the day
had been completed, he could talk to us the guests.

Little passed between us the first day, there was caution on both parts,
but as days went on many things were said, much was shared. First
was the account of our flying in a small plane, this delighted him
especially because he had flown his own plane to his various places
of business. We talked of how it would be when everything was straightened
out and we were allowed to take off again. Domingo flew the plane many
times in our little room, the exhiliration of becoming airborne, ~~wxraxbtbar~~
~~xxrbxxbx~~ surrounded by freedom in the air were bitter contrast to
this confinement. His face would be extatic as he simulated pushing
in the throttle and pulling back the wheel, and then the pain of realizing
and remembering that this he could not do now, would darken his face
for an instant until he could smile again and say this is what you will

APARTADO 8 · MANAGUA, NICARAGUA · CABLE: BLUEBROS

MCT   6   15 October, 1961

you will be doing soon, everything will be allright, they will let
you go soon, I am sure of it".

After several days and still no indication of any interest in Swenson
and myself, much less of letting us go, Domingo became more concerned.
"Don't tell me if you think you shouldn't but is there anything they
could possibly have on you". I had asked his advise, he wanted to
help me. He was considerably relieved when I answered that We
were completely clean, that they could not have anything on us. Again
his considered opinion that we would be out soon was reasurcing.

I never asked him what they had him in for. I knew he would tell me
if he had felt it wise. His spirit was so high, his mind so apparently
free for the problems and conderns of others, that I could not imagine
that he had fear of their proving anything serious against him.
At the same time, I knew that this kind of man could not but
be involved in some way in seeking the freedom of his country from
Fidel's tyrany.

After four days, I went through a most painful job of shaving with
a razor blade which had seen perhaps 30 shaves. I reasoned that I
should keep as much of my semblance of an innocent young man as
possible. Domingo's beard by that time was full, black and past the
stubble stage. He did not want to shave. He wanted you, Dona Martha
to see him with it. He said he thought he would be seeing you in
Miami in about two weeks. I knew not whether he really thought this,
but hopped that he knew something that I didn't that would make him
a free man inside those two weeks. In retrospect, I wonder if he
knew of the impending invasion and had that confidence in it, and knew
of its expected date. If not, this was merely more of his perfect aspect
of complete inocence and lack of involvment.

He told me of you and your children and it was of immense comfort to
him to know that you were safe. His sole concern seemed to be that
I impress on you the importance of your staying in Miami with the
children. Manuel Pugy, whose wife was upstairs in another cell and
whose children were in Havana, did not have Domingo's peace of mind
regarding his family.

In the later days, as Manuel "Yongo" became more open, he begged me
to tell him when the United States was going to take a positive stature
toward Fidel, when the necessary military campaign would begin. He
told me of the futility of the mountain and Guerilla operations and I

APARTADO 6 · MANAGUA, NICARAGUA · CABLE: BLUEBROS

MCT   7   15 October, 1961

agreed that any a full scale invasion was necessary. Domingo listened,
but did not offer anything. I had to give Yongo some encouragment.
I told him perhaps inside of two months months. To myself I resolved
to never rest, assuming I shoudd be released, until they and Cuba
were liberated.

I left Domingo on April 1 and finally reached the USA on April 4.
I had been with him nine days. He was still his ebulant self and still
solely responsible for the excellent moral that prevailed the room, but
his moments of thoughtful frustration and despair lasted somewhat longer.
Still, one had to watch him a great deal of the time to catch these feelings.
These last days disturbed me for him because I could see that he was
becoming more than nominally concerned. I reasoned and hopped that
this was solely due to his frustration at being cooped up for the extended
period of time. If he expected his fate, and with the perspective of time
of time and some knowledge of his involvment I can hardly think that he
could have expected anything else, or at least had faced the reality that
this was probable, this expectation was impossible to percieve, so brave,
generous and corageous his aspect.

On several evenings the magnificense of his voice would be transformed
to song, gay Cuban songs. At one time we had three others with extraordina
voices, a perfect quartet. The music was so lively that the guards would
repeatedly caution mix us to quiet down, but the spirit generated whx went
on in softer tones. Domingo aa was Cabo here to, leading the men,
playfully chastising those who would blemish the otherwise perfect harmony
or perfectly intended harmony, and then quieting them down when he felt
the guards had been pushed as far as expediante. . . . which was far
becasse the guards liked the musid too and were ammused that such
excellent sound and spirit could come from the hot packed room.

And then in between these rockus moments, some of them made durther
so by his clowning a dance, he would tell some of the other men of his
business of how the private enterprise system had worked and how it
had been wrecked. He would tell them of how the wages he had paid
would compare to those which the government was now paying. He told
of the 15 years of hard work , sometimes around the clock, to build his
business, the sacrifices that you, Dona Martha and he had made. And
then how it had been completely takensbxx away, even down to the pictures
of you and the children on his desk when the government walked in and
anowaced that nothing was to be removed, that all was now government
property. Now he had "nada, nada, mix nada", he laughed and joked

about this in a manner that all understood and appreciated.
The men who listened, and you can be sure this numbered them
all, were fascinated and better than ever understood the disaster
that Fidel had brought. The men were of all backgrounds, some
most modest, others of means and education. . . . they had never
had the problems and injustices explained and portrayed so candidly
and yet in a way that would have ammused even Fidel.

Then on a Sunday, someone brought a jar of instant Cafe Regil. After
extolling its virtues for several moments , the Cabo mixed it in with
the morning Cafe con Leche, it was his gift to all, never was there
a finer blend. Domingo was well pleased. In later times I could come
to Cuba, ask for the big "Regil" and he would introduce me to his family
and he would show me Cuba as it was going to be. His strength, all
of it that I had come to know, and his determination in his assertion,
left not the slightest doubt in my mind that this would become reality.
If he had any doubt, his superb control would not let it be evidenced.

As indications became prevelant that I would be released, his spirits
seemed to return to their level during the first days. I gave all the men
pieces of US change, the only thing I had, for thens their good luck.
I gave Domingo a quarter.

Domingo was in the water closet seeing to the water supply. He was
in for several minutes and then I walked in after him. We would not
be overheard there, if any place was safe. I told him I understood
what I had seen and experienced in that room, that I would not forget
it, that I would tell of it. I believe he understood the urgency , and
intensity of these simple things I had said. I believe this pleased him,
I believe he understood that if I got out, I would fight for the things he
was fighting for, that part of his urgent faith in Cuba's liberation,
had been emparted to me.

Word came that I was to be removed immediately. Domingo hurriedly
asked that I send back thxx my ball point pen maxindhxxt to the Cooperativeo
as indication that I had been freed. Domingo never recieved this because
the guards at my liberation point would not take it. This hurt me, but
I believe he could not have but sensed that kgxtxxxx Swenson and I got
out and I know this put his mind somewhat at peace. . . .he knew that
you would have my word of him and that you and the children would be
all right.

MCT   9   18 October, 1961

And so it was my privilege and honor to have known your husband.
I know of none that I regard more ~~xxxxx~~ highly. If this can serve to
bring you and your children closer to him in his last days, if it can serve
to tell you of a fraction of his greatness during the time I knew him

*the weight of his loss, however, would compared
to yours, will be partially eased. If it
can partially ease the weight his loss
has been to you, I will be infinitely
gratified.*

Yours always,

GLOSSARY

Al Qaeda
A loosely organized group of radical Islamist terrorists. They believe that a Christian-Jewish alliance is conspiring to destroy Islam. They are responsible for many bombings around the world, including the 1988 U.S. Embassy bombings, the 9/11/2001 attack on the World Trade Center in New York, and the 2002 bombing in Bali, Indonesia. Originally led by Osama Bin Laden, who was killed by U.S. Navy operatives in 2011. Bin Laden was succeeded by a radical fundamentalist Egyptian Ayman Al-Zawahiri.

Anarchy
Generally defined as a society without a structured public government, meaning that there are no set rules or morës to follow. Usually aligned with far left-wing ideology.

Austerity
Austerity, or "austerity measures" means policies whose goal is to reduce government budget deficits. The deficits in most cases arise from long-term socialistic regulation.

Bastiat, Claude Frédéric (1801-1850) was a French "classical liberal" (conservative or libertarian) theorist, political economist, and member of the French assembly.

Bay of Pigs
A failed invasion of Cuba by pro-American Cuban ex-patriots on April 17, 1961. The Cubans had worked with the CIA on the origination of the

plan. Conceived during the Eisenhower administration, it was adopted by President John F. Kennedy. The goal was to unseat Fidel Castro, after Castro's communist takeover from the Batista government. At the last minute, Kennedy withdrew air support which resulted in the slaughter or imprisonment of the Cuban ex-patriots who manned the invasion.

Berlin Wall

In 1961, the communist government of East Germany began to build an impenetrable wall between East and West Germany. The stated reason was to keep western "fascists" from entering East Berlin and corrupting the populace. The real reason was to stem the tide of East Germans defecting to West Germany. The wall stood for 28 years, separating families and blocking the right of East Germans to work in West Germany. On November 9, 1989, the head of the East German communist party announced that East Germans could once again travel as they wished to West Germany. Ecstatic crowds swarmed the wall, and began to demolish it with picks and axes. The Berlin Wall remains one of the most powerful symbols of the Cold War.

Bureaucracy

An administrative policy-making group of unelected government officials.

Capitalism (*see also* Free Enterprise)

An economic system in which trade, industry and the means of production are generated by private citizens with the goal of making profits in a market economy, which in turn increases the living standards of the society.

Central Bank

The central banking system in the U.S. is known as the Federal Reserve System (commonly known as "the Fed"), which is composed of 12 regional Federal Reserve Banks located in major cities throughout the country. The main tasks of the Federal Reserve are to supervise and regulate banks, implement monetary policy by buying and selling U.S. Treasury bonds and steer interest rates.

Centralization
In politics, concentration of a government's power (geographically, politically, economically) into a centralized government structure.

Classical Liberalism
A political philosophy with a primary emphasis on securing the freedom of the individual by limiting the power of the government. Classical Liberalists also support civil rights under the rule of law, private property rights, and *laissez-faire* economic policy. In Europe, someone deemed a "liberal" is often in essence a classic liberal, i.e., a conservative or libertarian by American standards.

C.I.A.
"Central Intelligence Agency." The CIA is "an independent agency responsible for providing national security intelligence to senior US policymakers." (CIA website)

Cold War
The "Cold War" was a long term geopolitical, ideological and economic struggle between the Soviet Union and the United States. The term came into use in 1947 when a journalist, Walter Lippman, published a book entitled *The Cold War*. It was a "cold" war because nuclear weapons were never used. Instead, there was an arms race between the countries, various military alliances, economic warfare, targeted trade embargos, propaganda and disinformation, espionage and counterespionage. The "war" cycled through high and low tension periods; a time of low tension was called "détente" ("an ending of tension"). Tensions increased just prior to the fall of the Berlin Wall and the collapse of the Soviet Union in 1991.

Collectivism

Collectivism is the opposite of individualism, and refers to any philosophic, political, religious, economic or social outlook that emphasizes the interdependence of all people, such as socialism/communism.

Collectivism, horizontal

Horizontal collectivism stresses collective decision-making among equal individuals and is usually based in decentralization and egalitarianism (such as a cooperative enterprise).

Collectivism, vertical

Vertical collectivism is based on hierarchical structures of power and on moral and cultural conformity and is therefore based on centralization and hierarchy.

Common Law

That part of English law derived from custom and judicial precedent, rather than statutes. Common law is the basis for most statutes in the United States, with the exception of Louisiana.

Common Ownership

In political philosophy this refers to joint ownership of property. Common ownership of the means of production is asserted (put into action) by communism and some forms of socialism. The ultimate end of this philosophy is that some work and some don't and those who don't get supported by those who do.

Communism

A classless, moneyless, stateless social order structured upon common ownership of the means of production, as well as a social, political and economic ideology and movement that aims at the establishment of this social order. Such a society takes away most human civil rights, and mires the population in a low-production, low-motivation mode. The government owns the means of production and there is little private property. For this reason, there is less motivation to be productive.

Company town
In a company town, a major industry builds housing nearby for its workers, and provides essential services such as employment and stores.

Competition
(In this book we are concerned with Economic Competition, rather than the rivalry for supremacy exhibited in professional sports, etc.) In economic competition, each actor strives to be the best, to provide the best product or service to the public. "Competition works well only if private property rights are protected and people are free to make contracts under the rule of law." (Wolfgang Kasper, professor emeritus of economics at the University of New South Wales, Australia.)

Conservatism
In the United States, conservatism originally was rooted in the American Revolution and its commitment to republicanism, sovereignty of the people, and the rights and liberties of the people. Currently, national conservatism is strongly focused on the family and traditional values. Economic conservatives (and libertarians) favor small government, low taxes, limited regulation and free enterprise. Conservatives also favor a strong military as the means to maintain freedom and order.

Corollary
Something that follows from something already proven. For example, increased taxation is a natural corollary to a new government spending program.

Crony capitalism is a term describing an economy in which success in business depends on close relationships between business people and government officials. It may be exhibited by favoritism in the distribution of legal permits, government grants, special tax breaks, or other forms of state interventionism.

Deep State
Members of the government bureaucracy who tend to maintain their positions of power and influence in the government regardless of changes of elected officials and changes of political control.

Deflation
A general decline in prices, often caused by a reduction in the supply of money or credit. Deflation can be caused also by a decrease in government, personal or investment spending. The opposite of inflation, deflation has the side effect of increased unemployment since there is a lower level of demand in the economy, which can lead to an economic depression. Central banks attempt to stop severe deflation, along with severe inflation, in an attempt to keep the excessive drop in prices to a minimum. (Investopedia)

Democracy
"Pure" democracy is government of the masses through direct operation. This system often results in ineffective government, since a large majority of people do not closely follow politics, are not adequately informed, and therefore vote on emotional bases, rather than merit. Minorities and their interests are not protected.

Economic Policy
Actions that governments take in the economic field, such as setting interest rates and government budget as well as regulating the labour market, national ownership, and other areas of government interventions. Other influences on economics include the International Monetary Fund (the World Bank), and positions and policies of political parties.

Economics
The study of the production, distribution and consumption of wealth in human society.

Egalitarianism
A belief in equality of outcomes, especially with respect to social, political, and economic affairs.

Elitism
Elitism is the belief or attitude that some individuals, should have more influence or authority than others. They believe they have extraordinary skills, abilities, or wisdom that render them especially fit to govern over others.

Friedrich Engels (1820-1895)
Co-author (with Karl Marx) of "The Communist Manifesto" and editor of "Das Capital," the foundation book on communism. Interestingly, while Engels preached against control of the proletariat by the economic elite, Engels' father was a successful businessman, and upon his death, Engels left his inherited millions to Karl Marx's daughters. Engels supported Karl Marx during his writing of the first volume of "Das Capital."

"Entitlement society"
This refers to a society where a substantial portion of the electorate believe they are "entitled" to certain "rights" to which they believe they have a claim, such as welfare benefits.

Entrepreneur
A person who conceives, organizes, promotes, and operates a business, assuming risk for the venture, usually with initiative and innovation.

Executive Order
An executive order is a directive from the executive branch of government (the President) without oversight or input from the legislative or judicial

branches of government. An executive order is within the constitutional authority of the Executive Branch to enforce laws passed by Congress.

Federal Reserve Board

The Federal Reserve Board is the governing body of the Federal Reserve System, which sets policy regarding the Federal Reserve discount rate (the rate at which banks may borrow from the Fed) and reserve requirements (the amount of money and liquid assets Federal Reserve member banks must hold or deposit with the Fed). The Board consists of 7 members appointed by the President and confirmed by the Senate.

Feudal Society

The organization of medieval Europe (5th – 15th century) into "feudalism," where land grants were given to the gentry (nobles) in exchange for fealty to the King. In turn, the nobles doled out land to the knights, and on the bottom rung were the serfs, who had no rights and worked the land basically as slaves.

Fixed Exchange Rate

A country's exchange rate regime under which the government or central bank ties the official exchange rate to another country's currency (or the price of gold). The purpose of a fixed exchange rate system is to maintain a country's currency value within a very narrow band. Also known as pegged exchange rate. From www.investopedia.com Fixed rates provide greater certainty for exporters and importers. This also helps the government maintain low inflation, which in the long run should keep interest rates down and stimulate increased trade and investment.

Founding Fathers

The statesmen, politicians and citizens who comprised the group responsible for the United States Constitution of 1787. There were 55 framers of the Constitution, although only 31 signed the actual document. Key among them were John Adams, Benjamin Franklin, Alexander Hamilton, John Jay, Thomas Jefferson, James Madison and George Washington.

"Free Enterprise"

Freedom of individuals and businesses to organize and operate in a competitive system without interference by government beyond the regulation necessary to protect the public interest and keep the national economy in balance. [*See also*, "Free Market"]

"Free Market"

A free market is a market economy in which the forces of supply and demand are not controlled by a government or other authority. [*See also*, "Free Enterprise]

FREEDOM (the highest ideal)

The right or power to think, speak or act as you wish, without restraint, and especially without government restriction.

Free Market Economy

In a "free" market economy, economic decisions and prices are decided by market forces rather than central planning. Individuals own resources and can allocate them in the way they choose. Investment, production and distribution decisions are based on supply and demand in the "market", and prices of goods and services are determined in a free price system. The opposite of a free market is a centrally planned economy (typical in socialist and communist countries), heavily regulated or controlled by a totalitarian government.

Futurist

Futurists (such as Herman Kahn and Max Singer) are scientists and political scientists whose goal is to research and predict future world trends and possibilities.

Hayek, Friedrich (F.A.) (1899-1992)

Friedrich August von Hayek, born in Austria-Hungary (but later of British citizenship) was an economist and philosopher best known for his defense of classical liberalism. The original principles of classical liberalism are now for the most part embodied in conservative beliefs. In 1974, Hayek shared the *Nobel Memorial Prize in Economic Sciences* (with Gunnar Myrdal) for his "pioneering work in the theory of money and economic fluctuations and ... penetrating analysis of the interdependence of economic, social and institutional phenomena."

Hierarchy
A system or organization in which people or groups are ranked one above the other according to status or authority.

Hyperinflation
Hyperinflation is a situation where the price increases are so out of control that the concept of inflation is meaningless. (Investopedia)

Impetus
A force that causes something (such as a process or activity) to be done or to become more active; a driving force.

Individualism
The moral stance, political philosophy, ideology, or social outlook that emphasizes the moral worth of the individual. Individualists promote the exercise of one's goals and desires and so value independence and self-reliance and advocate the interests of the individual should achieve precedence over the state or a social group, while opposing excessive external interference of individual lives by society or institutions such as the government.

Industrial Revolution
The Industrial Revolution involved a major improvement in manufacturing processes that caused significant changes all over the world. Up until that time, there was no way to mass produce articles. The later period included greater use of steam power and machine tools, as well as a switch from wood to coal fuel. The "second industrial revolution" is considered to be the period from around 1840 to the beginning of

World War I, when production lines came into being, along with steel and factory electrification.

Inflation

Inflation is the rate at which the general level of prices for goods and services is rising and, consequently, the purchasing power of currency is falling. Central banks attempt to limit inflation, and avoid deflation, in order to keep the economy running smoothly

Intellectual property rights

Legally protected creations of the mind. Expression is protected (e.g., books, music, art, etc.); ideas are not, with the exception of functional ideas that rise to the level of patentability.

International Monetary Fund

Founded in 1945 with 188 member countries to help with post World War II monetary policy, the IMF "provides policy advice and financing to members in economic difficulties and also works with developing nations to help them achieve macroeconomic stability and reduce poverty. The IMF provides policy advice and financing to members in economic difficulties and also works with developing nations to help them achieve macroeconomic stability and reduce poverty. The IMF supports its membership by providing:

- policy advice to governments and central banks based on analysis of economic trends and cross-country experiences;

- research, statistics, forecasts, and analysis based on tracking of global, regional, and individual economies and markets;

- loans to help countries overcome economic difficulties;

- concessional loans to help fight poverty in developing countries; and

- technical assistance and training to help countries improve the management of their economies." www.imf.org

ISIS (Islamic State of Syria and the Levant)
Formed in 2013, ISIS is a jihadi Salafist militant group, that was formerly part of Al Qaeda in Iraq. They are bitterly hostile to Western Civilization and their goal is worldwide domination and establishment of a borderless radical fundamentalist Islamic State.

Keynesian Economics
John Maynard Keynes (1883-1946) first articulated his theory of economics in his book *The General Theory of Employment, Interest and Money*, published in 1936. His theory promoted general (aggregate) spending, especially during recessions, which did not necessarily equate with the nation's output possibility but which was influenced by many factors. The noted economist Milton Friedman was critical of this theory, postulating that the public sector could not effectively police the private sector with fiscal policy. Although adopted by many capitalist governments, Keynesian theory lost favor in the 1970s, but enjoyed a resurgence during the recession of 2007-2008. However, most economists agree that government spending did not help much in the recent recession.

KGB (Komitet gosudarstvennoy bezopasnosti: "Committee for State Security")
The KGB was the main security agency for the Soviet Union from 1954 - 1991. The organization acted as internal security, intelligence and secret police. After the dissolution of the USSR in 1991, the KGB was split into the Federal Security Service and the Foreign Intelligence Service of the Russian Federation.

Khrushchev, Nikita
Khrushchev led the Soviet Russia as Premier during the heat of the Cold War, from 1958-1964. He instigated the Cuban Missile Crisis by placing nuclear warheads 90 miles from Florida. He approved construction

of the Berlin Wall, and is known for colorful speeches. During one such speech at the United Nations, he took off a shoe and pounded the podium with it.

Laissez-Faire (or *Laissez-Faire* Economics)
("Let it be" or "Leave it alone.)
An economic environment in which transactions between private parties are free from government restrictions, tariffs, and subsidies, with only enough regulations to protect private property rights.

Left-wing Liberalism
According to the Encyclopedia Britannica, "In the United States, liberalism is associated with the welfare-state policies of the New Deal program of the democratic administration of President Franklin D. Roosevelt, whereas in Europe it is more commonly associated with commitment to limited government and laissez-faire economic policies [*i.e., classical liberalism*]." [*See,*"Classical Liberalism."] In the U.S., liberals voice strong opposition to conservative positions and are known for enunciating strong emotional views that are often found not to be backed up by fact. They are for expanding spending and bigger government, seeking to gain control and power so that the populace is more dependent on the government for services.

Lenin, Vladimir (1880-1924) (birth name Vladimir Ilyich Ulyanov)
A Russian revolutionary, politician and political theorist, who led the bloody Bolshevik Revolution and helped create the communist Soviet Union, a totalitarian dictatorship where millions who opposed the government were killed.

Liberalism, Classical:
A political philosophy with a primary emphasis on securing the freedom of the individual by limiting the power of the government. Classical Liberalists also support civil rights under the rule of law, private property

rights, and laissez-faire economic policy. (Not to be confused with "Left-wing Liberalism")

Magna Carta of 1215

The Magna Carta, initially issued in Latin, was a document forced upon King John of England (seen by most as an evil King) by feudal Barons. The Magna Carta primarily guaranteed that no free man could be arrested without due cause, nor could lands be attacked by the King at random. It was more a document restraining the king's actions rather than a true declaration of independence. Even after King John's death, the Magna Carta remained as the basis for the "rule of law" doctrine, and was the source of vital legal concepts of the American Constitution and Bill of Rights, including "no taxation without representation" (the hue and cry against the Sugar Act of 1764, which preceded the Tea Party in Boston Harbor).

The "Market"

An arena (such as the American economic market) where the forces of supply and demand operate between individuals or entities, with minimal government intervention or restriction. (*See also*, Free Market Economy.)

Morës (mohr-ehz)

A term coined by William Graham Sumner (1840-1910), an early U.S. sociologist, to define behaviour that is considered right or wrong within a society or section of society, including aversion or adhesion to societal taboos.

Macroeconomics

The study of the structure and behaviour of the economy as a whole, rather than individual markets.

Marx, Karl Heinrich (1818-1883)

A German philosopher, economist, sociologist, historian, journalist and revolutionary socialist. Marx's theories about society, economics and politics — collectively known as <u>Marxism</u> — hold that human societies progress through <u>class struggle</u>: a conflict between an ownership class that controls production and a dispossessed labor class that provides labor for production. He called <u>capitalism</u> the "dictatorship of the <u>bourgeoisie</u>," believing it to be run by the wealthy classes for their own benefit; and he predicted that, like previous socioeconomic systems, capitalism would eventually self-destruct and be replaced by a new system: <u>socialism</u>. His prophecy has proved false. (*See* **Socialism**.)

Marxism
The political and economic theories of Karl Marx and Friedrich Engels, later developed by their followers to form the basis for the theory and practice of communism. The Marxist ideal of socialist production is to be based on the rational planning of use-values (a product is valued according to the labor hours required to produce it, not how much it is deemed to be worth) and coordinated [i.e., regulated] investment decisions to attain economic goals. As a result, theoretically the cyclical fluctuations that occur in a capitalist market economy will not be present in a socialist economy. The value of a good in socialism is its physical utility rather than its embodied labour, cost of production and exchange value as in a capitalist system. One of the primary goals of this book is to offer the facts, illustrations and historical events that disprove this theoretical model. It is interesting to note that Marx and Engels wrote very little on socialism and almost nothing on how the system was to be organized.

Moore's Law
Moore's Law (named after Gordon Moore, the co-founder of Fairchild Semiconductor and CEO of Intel) is the 1965 observation that the number of transistors in a dense integrated circuit doubles about every two years, which increases the speed at which progress is made.

Natural Liberty
The power to act as one sees fit without any restraint or control from outside force except for the laws of nature.

Objectivism
The belief that certain things, especially moral truths, exist independently of human knowledge or perception of them.

Oligarchy
Oligarchy is a form of power structure in which power effectively rests with a small number of people. These people could be distinguished by royalty or family ties, wealth, education, corporate standing or military control. Such states are often controlled by a few prominent families who typically pass their influence from one generation to the next. But inheritance is not a necessary condition for the application of this term.

Pluralism
A condition where political and economic power is broadly based in a society.

Populist Politics (Populism)
The political doctrine that supports the rights and powers of the common people in their struggle with the privileged elite. (Princeton University definition)

Paradox
A paradox is a statement that apparently contradicts itself and yet might be true. Most logical paradoxes are known to be invalid arguments but may be valuable in promoting critical thinking.

Property
Generally, something owned by someone. This can be a piece of land, jewellery, a book, an invention, etc.

Property Rights
Government-created laws or regulations regarding how an individual can control, transfer and benefit from property. Under economic theory, it is

only when there is strong enforcement of such rights that a high level of economic success will be achieved.

Reformation

A profound movement in Christianity of the 16th century where vast changes were made by the Pope to the practices of the Church. The movement also resulted in the formation of various Protestant denominations.

Republic

Government of the people through vesting authority in officials elected by the public.

Rhetoric

The art of discourse which attempts to inform, persuade or motivate people in a certain situation on a specific subject.

Rule of Law

The legal principle that a country should be ruled by legislation (laws), rather than arbitrary decisions by individual government officials. The World Justice Project defines such law as including the following principles:

1. "The government and its officials and agents as well as individuals and private entities are accountable under the law.

2. The laws are clear, publicized, stable, and just; are applied evenly; and protect fundamental rights, including the security of persons and property.

3. The process by which the laws are enacted, administered, and enforced is accessible, fair, and efficient.

4. Justice is delivered timely by competent, ethical, and independent representatives and neutrals who are of sufficient number, have

adequate resources, and reflect the makeup of the communities they serve."

For stability, laws should be based on constitutions that are difficult to subvert.

Satellite State
A political term referring to a country that is formally independent, but actually labors under heavy political and economic influence or control by another country, e.g., East Germany during the Cold War, which was under pressure and control of the Soviet Union.   Winston Churchill's "Iron Curtain" speech references such satellite dependency: "From Stettin in the Baltic, to Trieste in the Adriatic, an iron curtain has descended across the Continent. Behind the line lie all the capitals of the ancient states of Central and Eastern Europe – Warsaw, Berlin, Prague, Vienna, Budapest, Belgrade, Bucharest and Sofia, all of these famous cities and the populations around them, lie in what I must call the Soviet sphere, and all are subject in one form or another not only to Soviet influence, but to a very high and, in many cases, increasing measure of control from Moscow." James C. Humes, *The Wit & Wisdom of Winston Churchill.* Harper Collins (1994), at 131.

Serfdom
A term describing the form of bondage during the Middle Ages whereby serfs (peasants) were bound to the Lord of the manor they worked on. The manor was the primarily unit of feudal society, and serfs were bound legally, socially and economically. In return for their service, they were provided protection, justice and a right to work the fields for their own sustenance. They had few rights beyond that, and any children born to them were born into serfdom and were not free men.

Shock Jock
A radio disc jockey who says shocking or offensive things.

Singer, Max
A brilliant futurist and co-founder of The Hudson Institute. Author of "History of the Future."

Socialism
Socialism is an economic system characterized by social ownership of the means of production and co-operative management of the economy. A socialist economic system is based on government control and distribution of output, rather than on free markets. History has shown that socialism ultimately leads to communism, where the State owns all means of production and personal wealth is limited to the very few who are favored by the State.

Stagflation, (*stagnation* + *inflation*), is a term used in economics to describe a situation where the inflation rate is high, the economic growth rate slows down, and unemployment remains steadily high. It raises a dilemma for economic policy since actions designed to lower inflation may exacerbate unemployment, and vice versa. The term is generally attributed to a British politician who became chancellor of the exchequer in 1970, Iain Macleod, who coined the phrase in his speech to Parliament in 1965.

Stalin, Joseph (a code name meaning "man of steel"; birth name: Iosif (Joseph) Vissarionovich Dzhugashvili)(1878-1953).
Stalin was a communist leader who came from an abusive father and a mother who had to take in washing to sustain the family. Stalin was responsible for more deaths in Europe than those caused by the regimes of Mussolini, Hitler, Hirohito, Mao ZheDong and Pol Pot combined. His reputation is that he sacrificed soldiers at his whim, starved civilians, carried out mass executions and genocide of millions, all between the end of World War I and World War II. Following World War II, he continued with his repressive regime, executing thousands, exiling others, censoring the arts. After his death, he was later renounced by Khruschev for "crimes against the Party" and building a cult following.

Statism/Statist
Merriam-Webster says that statism is concentration of economic controls and planning in the hands of a highly centralized government often extending to government ownership of industry. A statist is someone who supports statism.

Totalitarianism
A political system in which the state holds total authority over the society and seeks to control all aspects of public and private life. Both Naziism and Socialism/Communism are examples of totalitarian governments, and both derive from the same roots.

Traditional Values
Those beliefs, moral codes, and morës that are passed down from generation to generation within a culture, subculture or community.

Victorian Era
In British history, the Victorian Era covered the period of Queen Victoria's reign from 1837 to 1901. It was a long period of peace and prosperity for Britain, and was marked by a highly moralistic society with straight-laced manners.

Voltaire (1694-1778)
A French enlightenment historian and philosopher.

Wealth
A measure of the value of all of the assets of worth owned by a person, community, company or country. When Adam Smith wrote "The Wealth of Nations," he clarified that by "wealth" he meant the well-being of people.

"Work Ethic"
A belief in the benefit of working in order to contribute to one's self and one's family in addition to one's community or society in general, and the

confidence that such productive work helps to build character. "Work ethics" include the qualities of honesty and accountability.

The World Bank
The World Bank, established in 1944 and headquartered in Washington, D.C., provides financial and technical assistance to developing countries. Their stated mission was to end extreme poverty within a generation and boost shared prosperity.

World Trade Center Disaster ("9/11")
The term "9/11" refers to the events that took place in New York City on September 11, 2001, when fanatic Muslim extremists hijacked 4 commercial airplanes and crashed them into the two towers of the World Trade Center, into the Pentagon, and into a field in Shanksville, Pennsylvania. The plane that crashed in Shanksville was thought to be heading to the Capitol Building, but was thwarted by the passengers and crashed prematurely into a vacant field, savings many lives. 9/11 is considered the beginning of the "War on Terror," and was followed by the invasion of Iraq and Afghanistan, where the fanatics were being trained. Their goal was the destruction of America.

Zero-sum game
Where gains and losses are equal and the final calculation is zero.

BIBLIOGRAPHY

Ali, Ayaan Hirsi. *Infidel*. New York: Free Press (Simon and Shuster), 2007.

Anonymous, *Nine Commentaries on the Communist Party*. Mountain View, CA: Broad Press, 2004.

Bernstein, R.B. *The Founding Fathers Reconsidered*. Oxford/New York: Oxford University Press, 2009.

Blight, James G., editor, and Peter Cornbluh. *Politics of Illusion*. Boulder, CO: Lynne Rienner Publishers, 1998.

Carswell, Douglas. *The End of Politics*. London: Biteback Publishing, 2012.

Dalberg-Acton, John Emerick Edward. *Essays in the History of Liberty*. Cambridge: Cambridge University Press, 1985.

_____ *The History of Freedom*. London: The Acton Institute, 1993.

D'Souza, Dinesh. *The Roots of Obama's Rage*. Wash., D.C.: Regnery Publishing, 2010.

Friedman, Milton. *Capitalism and Freedom*. Chicago: The University of Chicago Press, 1962.

_____. *Why Government is the Problem*. Stanford, CA: Hoover Institution on War, Revolution and Peace, Stanford University, 1993.

Friedman, Milton and Rose Friedman. *Free to Choose: A Personal Statement*. New York: Houghton Mifflin Harcourt, 1980.

[319]Gilder, George. *Knowledge and Power*. Wash. D.C.: Regnery Publishing, 2013.

Gingrich, Newt. *Winning the Future*. Wash., D.C.: Regnery Publishing: 2005.

_____ *A Nation Like No Other*. Wash., D.C.: Regnery Publishing: 2011.

Hannan, Daniel. *The New Road to Serfdom*. New York: Broadside Books (Harper Collins), 2010.

_____ *Why American Must Not Follow Europe*. New York: Encounter Broadsides, 2011.

_____ *Inventing Freedom*. New York: Broadside Books (Harper Collins), 2013.

Hayek, F.A. *The Constitution of Liberty*. Chicago: The University of Chicago Press, 1960.

_____*The Road to Serfdom*. Chicago: The University of Chicago Press, 2007.

---

319 Geyer, Georgie Ann. *Guerrilla Prince: The Untold Story of Fidel Castro*. New York: Little, Brown & Company, 1991.

BIBLIOGRAPHY

_____ *The Fatal Conceit: The Errors of Socialism.* Chicago: The University of Chicago Press, 1989.

Hazlitt, Henry. *Economics in One Lesson.* New York: Three Rivers Press (Crown Publishing Group), 1962.

Hicks, Alexander. *Social Democracy and Welfare Capitalism.* Ithaca, NY: Cornell University Press, 1999.

Horowitz, David. *Barack Obama's Rules for Revolution.* Sherman Oaks, CA: David Horowitz Freedom Center, 2009.

Humes, James C. *The Wit & Wisdom of Winston Churchill.* New York: Harper Collins, 1994.

Kent, Neil. *A Concise History of Sweden.* Cambridge, U.K.: Cambridge University Press, 2008.

Keynes, John Maynard; *The General Theory of Employment, Interest, and Money.* NY: Harcourt, Brace & Company, 1935.

Kornai, Janos and Stephan Haggard and Robert R. Kaufman, *Reforming the State: Fiscal and Welfare Reform in Post-socialist Countries.* Cambridge: Cambridge University Press, 2001.

Krauthammer, Charles. *Things That Matter.* New York: Crown Forum Books, 2013.

Lederer, Richard and Caroline McCullagh. American Trivia: What We All Should Know About U.S. History, Culture & Geography. Layton, UT: Gibbs/Smith, 2012.

Luntz, Dr. Frank. *Words That Work.* New York: Hyperion Books, 2007.

Mamet, David. *The Secret Knowledge.* New York: Sentinel/Penguin Books (USA), 2011.

McClanahan, Brian, Ph.D. *The Politically Incorrect Guide to The Founding Fathers.* Wash., DC: Regnery Publishing, 2009.

Meyer, Henning and Jonathan Butherford, editors. *The Future of European Social Democracy.*

Murray, Charles. *American Exceptionalism: An Experiment in History.* Wash. D.C.: AEI Press, 2013. Palgrave Macmillan. Hampshire: 2012.

Mises, Ludwig von. *Money, Method and the Market Process.* Auburn, AL: Ludwig Von Mises Institute, 2012.

_____. *The Anti-Capitalist Mentality.* The Ludwig von Mises Society, 1978.

_____ . *The Theory of Money & Credit.* Seattle: Pacific Publishing Studio, 2010.

Paine, Thomas. *Common Sense, Rights of Man.* New York: First Signet Classics, New American Library (Penguin Classics), 2003.

Plimer, Ian. *Heaven and Earth: Global warming, the missing science.* Lanham, Md: Taylor Trade Publishing, 2009.

Pritchitko, David L. Marxism. *The Concise Encyclopedia of Economics.* Indianapolis: Liberty Fund, 2008.

Rand, Ayn. Capitalism: The Unknown Ideal. New York: New American Library (Penguin), 1967.

Reynolds, Glenn Harlan. *The New School.* New York: Encounter Books, 2014.

Rossiter, Clinton. *The Federalist Papers.* New York: Signet Classic, 2003.

Sejersted, Francis. *The Age of Social Democracy.* Princeton, NJ: Princeton University Press, 2011.

Singer, Max, *History of the Future.* Lanham, Md: Lexington Books, 2011.

Sirico, Rev. Robert A. *Defending the Free Market.* Washington, D.C.: Regnery, 2012.

Smith, Adam. *The Wealth of Nations.* New York: Bantam Classic Edition, 2003.

Taleb, Nassim Nicholas. *The Black Swan: The Import of the Highly Improbable.* New York: Random House, Trade Paperback, 2010.

Wapshott, Nicholas. *Keynes/Hayek: The Clash That Defined Modern Economics.* New York: W.W. Norton, 2011.

Weber, Max. *The Protestant Ethic and the "Spirit" of Capitalism.* New York: Penguin Books, 2002.

Williamson, Kevin D. *The Dependency Agenda.* New York: Encounter/Broadside, 2012.

_____.*The Politically Incorrect Guide to Socialism.* Wash., D.C.: Regnery Publishing, 2011.

CPSIA information can be obtained
at www.ICGtesting.com
Printed in the USA
BVHW041300111121
621376BV00008B/89/J

9 781641 116312